Creating Transformational Metaphors

Marilyn Atkinson

Copyright © 2013 by Exalon Publishing, LTD

Cover background art by Christopher Redmond.

All rights reserved. No portion of this book may be reproduced, by any process or technique, without the express consent of the publisher.

ISBN-978-0-9783704-3-5

First published in 2013.

Printed in Canada.

The paper used in this book complies with the Permanent Paper Standard issued by the National Standards Organization (Z39.48-1984).

10 9 8 7 6 5 4 3 2 1

Contents

Dedication i
Acknowledgment ii

Preface 1
Consciousness Metaphors:
Vehicles for Transformative Learning 1
    Why Use the Approach of Metaphor? 3
    The Stories in This Book 4
    The Meditations in This Book 5
    Books I and II 5

Chapter 1 7
Finding the Secret Door 7
    Life on the Balance Beam 8
    What is a Metaphor? What is a 'Meta' for? 9
    Einstein on the Porch 10
    What Creates Transformation in Our Metaphors? 11
    Grandmother and the Boxes 12
    Create Anything—Tell Stories 13
    Milton and the Runaway Horse 14
    Exploring the Process of Holistic Awareness 15
    Lining Up Joy in Three Small Steps 15

Chapter 2 17
Identity Explorations, Tribulation, and Discovery 17
    The Surfer From Beijing 18
    Moving Beyond Identity as Tribulation 19
    The Dynamics 20
    Gifts of Consciousness 21
    Margaret's Story: The Choice to Have Huntington's 22
    A Pilgrim In The World 25

Chapter 3 27
Seeding Metaphoric Landscapes 27
    Scripted Emotions = Previously Recorded Conclusions 28
    Beyond the Death Mask 29
    Opening Pathways With Stories of Self-Realization 31

The Russian Radio 32
Creating Inner Gardens Using Open-Ended Questions 33
Marie and the Shock Treatments 34
Listening to Inner Knowledge 37
Red-Haired Men 39

Chapter 4 41
Why Do Humans Suffer? 41
Step Beyond Metaphoric Suffering to Enlightened Awareness 42
The Drunkard From Chelyabinsk 44
In Your Secret Heart: A Meditation 44
The Story of Victor Frankl 45
The Process of Creating Purpose 46
The Life of David Rigmore 47
The Hero's Journey 50

Chapter 5 53
Transforming Death: Stories to Move Beyond Suffering 53
Become Your 'Values Mind' 54
Solution-Focused Alchemy: The Tonglin Monk 56
Great 'Metaphor Makers' Create Alchemy 56
Develop Transformational Vision—Tell Stories 58
The River Crossing 59
Designing a Transformational Reality 62
The Story of Uriah Millard 63
Kayaking Images and the Heartbeat of Life 66
The Bengal Tiger Under the Bed 67
Washing Away Entitlement: A Meditation 68

Chapter 6 69
Connecting to Inner Truth 69
Building a New Mind 70
What mind do you wish to inhabit today? 70
The Significant Power of Promising 71
The Grand Canyon Wall 72
Promising Brings Results 73
Helen Keller: How to Create a 'Human' Mind 74
King Midas and True Value 75
The Shift to Personal Development 76
Mohandas Gandhi and Finding Forgiveness 77

- Be With Each Other 78
- Suffer Self-Knowledge 79
- *St. Francis and the Leper* 79

Chapter 7 81
- Integrity and Commitment 81
  - *Pointing Over the Fence: Declaring 100% Commitment* 82
  - Metaphors That Point 82
  - Emotional Renewal to Positive Energy 83
  - *The Flow of Vision: Building the Russian 'Town'* 84
  - How People Grow New Capacities 87
  - *The 'Teddy Bears Picnic'* 87

Chapter 8 91
- Your 'Integrity-Identity' As a Field of Consciousness 91
  - *What Is Integrity? Abraham Lincoln's Choice!* 92
  - Expanding Identity—Who Are We? 92
  - *The Man in the Red Jacket* 93
  - Bring Down the Wall 96
  - *True Human Potential: The Great Wall of China* 97
  - Sustainable Planet 98

Chapter 9 101
- Life's Great Gifts: Courage and Determination 101
  - Frame Your Strongest Identity 102
  - *The Story of Karl Wallenda* 104
  - Self-Mastery Coaching Through the Metaphor Story 106
  - *Coyotes in the Superstition Mountains* 107
  - *Living in a World Full of Criticism* 110
  - Self-Design Questions 113
  - *Becoming Cleopatra for the Crisis: Flexibility Coaching* ... 114
  - *Learning How To Walk* 116
  - Designing Deep Renewal 116

Chapter 10 119
- Teamwork and Transformation 119
  - *Breakthrough on the Trans-Canada Highway:*
  - *The Trucker and the Hitchhiker* 120
  - Pondering a Metaphor Into Life 123
  - How Do We Build 100% Commitment? 124
  - *Can We Follow the Track?* 125

    Life's Companions: A Short Exercise 127
    Getting Over the Fence 128
    Team Humanity—Getting Over The Fence 130
    A Story Called "Failing Forward" 130

Chapter 11 131
Friendship and Love 131
    Link People to Deep Principles 132
    Esref, the Blind Painter… the Flow of Vision 133
    Create With Principles and Punch Lines 134
    Punch Line Questions Call Us to the Quest 135
    The Story of Jacob's Ladder: Renew Your Energy! 136
    Milton Erickson's Principles 137
    Milton and George 137
    Rites of Passage 140
    Catching Planes: The Wonder of Just in Time 141
    Love Expands Beyond Emotion 142
    Mamma Mia and Rumi 144
    What Kinds of Principles Are Transformational? 146
    Mother Teresa's Rules 146
    Create Presence 147
    The Story of Tommy the Hermit 148
    Unbroken Wholeness: A Meditation 151

Chapter 12 153
Soaring With Synchronicity 153
    Beyond Belief: The Power of Synchronicity 154
    Identity as a Field of Consciousness 156
    The Cave 157
    Use Open-Ended Questions as Punch Lines 160
    The Eagle 161
    A Meditation—Catching the Breath of the Universe:
    Big and Small 163

Chapter 13 167
Awareness, Presence, and Wisdom 167
    The Solution-Focused Power of Gratitude 168
    The Village of Shining Moments 169
    The Meaning of 'Field Awareness' 170
    The Flute Player 171

Value Awareness 173
Create Your Own Travel Jar 174
Develop Field Awareness As You Tell Your Tale 176
The Larry Walter's Story 177
What is a metaphor? 178

Dedication

I dedicate this book to the storytelling playfulness of Milton Erickson, whose metaphoric descriptions of life development, awareness, vision, and wisdom have expanded my storytelling courage.

Marilyn Atkinson

Acknowledgment

This book has been a joy to create. The writing has been easy. The process has been like hiking on a summer day—full of discoveries and delights. The stories themselves have been part of my life and its unfolding over 50 years, and so my thank-yous go out to 50 years' worth of friends and companions. Thank you to everyone, whose input helped my life stories to unfold.

Specifically, I want to send thank-yous to the wonderful staff of various Erickson College communities in 44 countries. The stories have been tested with participants in so many terrific courses organized worldwide.

I particularly want to thank my assistants, typists, cover designers, and visionary layout people. Special thank-yous go to Alexandra Ivanova, Gale Leitch, and Maryanne Renzette, who assisted me to keep the process alive during complex multi-country teaching assignments. Gale's edits helped the book's flow; Alexandra's and Gale's cover ideas focused my creative attention; and Maryanne's early enthusiasm convinced me to keep moving.

Layout kudos go to Gale, whose fine work has produced enjoyable reading pages for us all.

In gratitude to the team effort,

Marilyn Atkinson
November 2013

Preface

Consciousness Metaphors: Vehicles for Transformative Learning

As a speaker, you possess a powerful tool for communication and motivation. Learn to use advanced metaphors to link people to the key principles that inspire, open, and deeply expand their awareness. With metaphors of mind expansion, you can assist others to learn to move into self-trust in their inner exploration and discovery processes.

Imagine that your values are like thermals—gentle rising currents of warm air. With a transformational metaphor, we are building a story about inner life that allows us to expansively rise up on this inner thermal elevator, into the wonderful warmth of these values.

Our basic ability to look at life and be pleased with our perceptions is like the glider rising in the thermal current. We respond naturally and without fear, as the story unfolds. Metaphors powerfully assist this process, so that people feel their deep values and see a transformative vision for themselves—**in the moment**—and through the story we are telling!

Consciousness metaphors, what you will discover in this manual, are stories that both 'show' and 'do' the expansion of self-awareness in the telling. They present an event or example that allows us to identify with a person who takes a large step forward.

The Sanskrit language includes 23 different words for consciousness, whereas the English language has only one. A Consciousness metaphor is designed to refine and develop new avenues for consciousness. The language of metaphor provides its own 'Sanskrit' so to speak, enlarging the lexicon of awareness. You discover a refined perception that may be outside your normal, daily range. This assists people to widen their awareness in new ways—like learning new words and images for difficult shared experiences. We develop expanded perceptions that allow for deeper and more meaningful communication. We learn to engage again, like a small child.

A consciousness metaphor is often a story about someone in the process of self-discovery who takes a risky, major jump in his or her development. **As we participate in such a story, valuable transformations occur.** We tend to associate with the visuals and values of such metaphors, and have life-expanding experiences. We listen to ourselves and become more self-aware.

We need embodied experiences to make our own inner knowledge come alive in terms of clear, aligned self-discoveries that we can recognize and express. Such stories allow us to develop and expand our consciousness—our vision and value awareness.

Human beings are associative. Metaphors assist us to dive into relational, full-bodied associative experiencing… as if into a deep pool of self-knowledge. We then add in the ability to think more effectively about our own life journey. We float to the surface of our life in a different pool. Through the story we can re-associate with and *feel* our core values.

Why Use the Approach of Metaphor?

Our lives can easily become fragmented by self-imagined walls. Suffering often provides an immediate primary awareness of this, when people suddenly discover they have become isolated within their own private 'radio band.'

Personal suffering is also metaphoric, but tends to produce a tightening tale—a sad story that closes us in! As we build transformational metaphors, we assist others to build strong new 'identity structures'—like cabins with wide windows, yet built to weather the storm.

With a consciousness metaphor, we often begin with the recognition of false boundaries. We present an individual who is suffering, and through storytelling we show how intelligent insight begins to emerge.

We humans need to study our suffering so that we can listen to it, enter it, try it on, question it effectively, and most importantly, learn to live *beyond* it. A metaphor can be used to remind us that it is possible to find a pathway through and beyond the old fragmentation patterns. We relax and once again begin to explore what we truly want. We now design for ourselves an open 'cabin for all seasons,' but built for stormy weather too. We rebuild the mind for choice and change.

A consciousness metaphor assists us in recognizing and responding to the internal maps and messages of people with whom we struggle for understanding. It also metaphorically assists us in listening to our own internal messages and maps, but *only* as messages and maps. In other words, we are enhancing our capacity for effective choice, no longer believing in the 'self difficulty' story.

With our stories, we assist people to explore important aspects of self-awareness. Our metaphoric mind is a hologramatic structure linking into both our communal intelligence and group awareness. You can move beyond your small 'radio band' of awareness and study the whole radio wave transmission system. You discover how to turn the dial, moving to wider *choice* in your life.

Different kinds of consciousness metaphors can be designed to open different distinctions, states, abilities, and awareness qualities, much like a 'weatherman' who studies approaching weather systems can assist you to choose appropriate clothing for your day's outing. They show people some key markers for the qualities of consciousness and awareness through which they, and others around them, may be passing. As you learn to create consciousness metaphors, you enhance your skills in engaging your own multiple-level life awareness.

The **thinking/planning function** and the **emotional function** come together through metaphor. We can create communal experiences as we create communal images for people. This reminds them of what they want to learn and give their energy to.

With a consciousness metaphor:
- We learn to share our experiences in a way that can create similar successes with others. We show how people learn and grow.
- Through the story, we discover how to open up to other people, even strangers, and see them as being like ourselves.
- We can, more effectively, speak to old emotional constrictions and assist others to move past old negative emotions. We can demonstrate these fear habits in our stories and metaphorically show how to move beyond them.
- Metaphors allow us to connect to others, and their experiences more freely. Metaphorically, we learn how to speak to deep experience.

We learn the steps in making a change that is paradoxically both painful and liberating.

The Stories in This Book

Inside our own effective story, we discover the way that intuitive **associative** processes operate **well**. Our stories provide an operative theatre for exploring our life of value and sharing it with others.

Any small story, or even an example that features a value image strong enough to captivate attention, can become a doorway to the inner potential of your listeners. We need to follow a few basic principles for that to happen.

I have taken time to collect multiple kinds of stories, my own and others, that allow the development of transformational thinking. You will find that some stories collected here create that result. Notice your inner response as you experience them.

There are about 30 metaphors, large and small, in the manual. Many of them have been designed for coaches. Explore them as a storyteller yourself, and use them as vehicles for personal pondering. Then, find your own wonderful metaphoric range and build your own examples.

The Meditations in This Book

This book includes some small, contemplative exercises and meditations that, like the stories, will easily awaken transformative potential when you practice them or even just imagine them. Use them for their 'joy potential' and create variations of your own. In Book II, to follow, I will also expand on metaphoric meditation development.

Books I and II

This is Book I in a pair of books on metaphoric expression. Book I is about the core elements of using a story for value development. Book II, next, is about storytelling techniques and practical engagement aids. It is about designing the physical process of a storytelling episode for a particular group of people.

In this book, Book I, you will learn how to activate and expand transformational values as experiences for people. You will discover ways to turn these into principles as you tell your story. In Book II of this series, we will explore multiple storytelling techniques and methodologies. This includes 'four quadrant' storytelling.

Chapter 1

Finding the Secret Door

In order to find out who you are,
Become a pole-vaulter: go over the bar.
In order to fly to the opposite side,
Let go of the pole and enjoy the ride!

—Marilyn Atkinson

Life on the Balance Beam

We live life on a balance beam of creative awareness: on one side sleepy oblivion, and on the other erratic driven obsession. Maintaining the balance beam of awareness reminds me of a special moment with my two grandchildren. Near Vancouver, British Columbia, is a suspension bridge that sits over a deep canyon gorge. This is a beautiful spot, with large cedars and hemlock trees on opposite cliffs and a sparkling river that splashes over rocks far below. Eagles circle far above. The Capilano River wends its way between high rocky points, and the tiny suspended footbridge seems to hang between here and eternity. I had last visited this bridge when I was just seven.

Mid-crossing, my 7-year-old granddaughter, Sage, and I looked down at the canyon as I answered her questions. "I was once here when I was seven, just like you," I tell her. "Maybe someday you will visit this spot with your own 7-year-old granddaughter." She gravely contemplated this idea.

Creative thinking emerges for all of us with overview. Time observation is particularly interesting. The children and I wonder about 'the future times' that might emerge on the bridge of awareness. Briefly, I think of the multiple generations of people who may have visited this spot over the last 10,000 years, and their thoughts of the magnificent canyon gorge.

Imagination peaks my interest and my mind swirls back, wondering about the eons of time required to cut the canyon itself. I reflect that many kinds of eyes may have looked out on this canyon over millions of years, and now these eyes see the same spot, as the canyon manifests its twenty-first century face. I now share this idea with my two grandchildren, who stop for a moment and look at the canyon with my 'through-time' vision. We all look through the 'eyes of time' at the incredible canyon view.

Now my 10-year-old grandson, Ross, decides to find a stone and to throw it into the canyon, "Just to make it different!" Looking

> carefully under bushes, he finds just the right stone and moves to the middle of the bridge. Checking that I am watching, he ceremoniously pitches it down to the river far below. **We all want to leave a mark on eternity.**
>
> The suspension bridge swings between two banks in the same way as we human beings learn to create balance—swinging between the paradoxes of our lives. We sustain the paradox by finding humor and trust in all the various aspects of our human journey.
>
> Sustainable balance becomes possible when we declare to ourselves that all aspects of the journey are worthy of true satisfaction. We learn to tell stories to share this with others. We declare that all aspects of the journey are valuable, and life becomes precious. The learning becomes a braid of learnings and we enter the flow of true satisfaction. **We all want to leave a mark on eternity.**

What is a Metaphor? What is a 'Meta' for?

Metaphors are doorways—wonderful integrative doorways providing huge transformational potential. They allow us to pass through and traverse beyond self-deception into areas of truthful mindscapes—perhaps to a place where we often dare not to go. Like a traveller transported to the moon, we get to view, walk, touch, and examine all of life's elements in a way that is fresh. We see from a new perspective. Through this wonderful doorway, we move past a *transformational threshold* into another deeper understanding of what it means to be human.

Think about the word itself, *metaphor*. What is the use of a 'meta' viewpoint? The prefix *meta* means "over and beyond," as in *'one step beyond any reality.'* One step beyond any reality is a story about that reality… it is a metaphor!

The concept of 'meta' works in many language examples:
- One step beyond physics is **metaphysics**.
- One step beyond a caterpillar, the butterfly emerges through **metamorphosis**.

In other words, one step beyond any model of anything, we can discover or create a '**meta model**.' This means that a major function of a metaphor is to step beyond any belief or assumption and lead the listener or reader to achieve a larger viewpoint.

What makes metaphors exceptional transformational doorways is that they can also assist us to associate into our deep values. Through a powerful metaphor, we can remember our values deeply and on a physical plane of experience.

The word *remember* itself is indicative. *Re-member* means "re-embodiment." We easily step into, feel, embody, and sense through the nervous system as we identify with a powerful story. This means that we formulate our identity from our kinesthetic and physical experiences of these values, thereby creating an expanded '*value connection*' throughout our body. A strong metaphor can create long-term value stabilization through this inner power, moving people physically and emotionally into renewed personal joy and energy toward their life's purpose.

Einstein on the Porch

A reporter from a scientific journal called and requested an interview with Einstein for a special article in their publication on "Great Questions from Great Scientists."

Dr. Einstein agreed and the reporter arrived at Einstein's home in the last moments of daylight. He found Einstein seated in a rocking chair on his porch puffing on a well-worn pipe and watching the red sunset.

"I have only one question to ask you, Dr. Einstein," said the reporter, a bright and nervous young man with a notebook. "This is the key question we are asking every scientist we can find. The question is: 'What is the most important question that a scientist can ask?'"

Envision silver mop-top Einstein, on the porch in his rocking chair with his eyes twinkling. "That is a great question, young man, and it

> *deserves a serious answer,"* he said. With that he commenced to rock slowly on his chair and puff on his aged pipe.
>
> The elderly Einstein stretched back and thought for ten minutes. He remained silent, and deep in thought for another few minutes, while the reporter waited expectantly for some significant mathematical formula or quantum hypothesis.
>
> The answer that the reporter received instead has had the world thinking carefully ever since. *"Young man,"* Einstein said gravely, *"the most important question that **any** person can ask is whether or not the universe is a friendly place."*
>
> *"What do you mean?"* replied the reporter. *"How can **that** be the most important question?"*
>
> Einstein responded solemnly, *"The answer we find determines what we do with our lives. If the universe is a friendly place, we will spend our time building bridges. Otherwise, people use all their time to build walls. We decide!"*

What Creates Transformation in Our Metaphors?

Key principles are at play with a transformational story.

First: The image needs to represent an aspect that is *'whole and complete'* in some way—a whole person, a whole life, a whole value, or perhaps 100% commitment.

Second: We need to observe from an *observer viewpoint* or *coach position*, thereby seeing the transformation potential in the events. Through our *story*, we call the listeners to join this coach position so that a deep *'coach's overview'* of the event can occur. At this point, we move outside the *'action'* of the story to the coach position so that we may then overview the various *'viewpoints'* inside our event. When a coach position exists, so does our capacity for transformational experience. As we *tell our story*, our gestures and expressions all assist to build this transformational potential.

Third: We need to show the movement of transformation: visually, kinesthetically, and auditorily (in our tone), as well as through the storyline. We need to make the forward movement compelling and associative so that people experience it '*in the bones.*' This allows us to create an alignment and deep *reorganization of self-awareness* to expand to the wider viewpoint. We point to the event from a viewer's position.

Grandmother and the Boxes

My grandmother loved her household things: her furniture, her bedroom suite, and her dishes. I played on her furniture as a child and knew every piece well.

When she was in her late eighties, she lay ill for many days, with pneumonia. She was very frail at this point, so her daughters telephoned the rest of the family to come and see her, convinced she was at the end of her life. I arrived from a trip, drove most of the night, and entered her home in the early morning. She had had a severe bout of pneumonia, and her daughters and doctors believed it would be her end.

When I first saw her, she had just awakened. The early morning sun poured through the windows. My tired aunts told me that her fever had broken late the day before, that she had slept well, and that it looked like she would survive. The worst of the pneumonia was over.

She lay back on the pillow, and happily drank the tea that her daughter brought while she whispered hello to me. We loved each other, and it was an eager visit. I was excited to see that it was like the dawning of a new day of real life for her. She was also surprised that she was still alive and said so. "How interesting," she whispered. "They said I would die and here I am still!" Through crisis, life sometimes offers us new eyes to see through and for Grandma, on this morning, her life was an amazing blessing.

She slowly focused. She was in her bedroom filled with her special bedroom furniture.

She looked at it with eyes of renewal and laughed and joked with me. "They are boxes, just boxes," she said, waving her hand and indicating her precious furniture and lifetime possessions.

> *Then she looked at her ancient, withered hands with gratitude. "I can still move everything," she announced, as if surprised. "They still work! Good hands through the years!" Again she chuckled, and added, "Well, what is a body anyway? It is interesting! Have you noticed, Marilyn, that, from inside, we are the same from the moment we are born until the day we die? The body is just a shell, like this furniture—just another box. Maybe the self-image changes, but not our inner self."*
>
> *Grandma paused and relaxed. She warmly entered the spacious, observational emptiness between all thoughts. Quantum physicists call this the implicate order, the ongoing wave frequency between all 'electrons,' all particles. This is the 'sameness' that forms the background to all differences: the unbroken wholeness that connects us all. I entered the warm space with her, and we sat together for half an hour.*
>
> *Later, in a tone of gratitude, she remarked again: "We are really exactly the same as when we first become aware. I am the same as when I was two years old." It was a major realization for her. "Wonderful," she said, feeling the flow of awareness and discovery while sipping her tea.*
>
> *What a wonderful thing to feel the spacious awareness; consciousness as wholeness.* **Spacious awareness**, *the sameness between us all. Here is Grandma's recipe for joy: Take half an hour; abide in this awareness. Sip your tea, and simply feel the wonder of it all!*

Create Anything—Tell Stories

One powerful purpose of metaphors is to find one's own *deep wisdom* and share it as a gift in the form of a story—as opposed to presenting it as a piece of advice. We each have a natural affinity for tapping into our own pool of profound inner knowledge. Your story will become your springboard to dive into that pool of inspiration.

Start with your own energetic *story of self-development*. Tap into what is emerging through your own unique life. Share your values, key events, discoveries, and what it all means to you, by diving into one moment's experience from your past and transforming it into a riveting story to share with other people. Share your visions and questions. What doors can you now open for others to walk through?

Milton and the Runaway Horse

Milton Erickson used to tell his students about life on a Minnesota farm where he grew up with his younger brothers and sisters.

One afternoon, as Milton and the children were playing in the barnyard, a strange horse—large, lively, and red—trotted down the driveway. It quickly passed the children, and proceeded to drink at the water trough.

The children were astounded. Milton, who was the oldest, decided to try a daredevil feat. Climbing gently up the water trough beside the horse, he eased himself down onto the horse's back. The horse seemed briefly surprised and then continued to drink.

When the horse finished drinking, Milton pulled on its thick red mane and, using his knees, urged it to move. Following his guide, the horse trotted back up the driveway. At the top of the lane, the horse hesitated and Milton waited. Finally, the horse chose a direction and Milton used his knees to urge him forward.

Four hours later, in a totally different area of the valley, a sun-burned farmer looked up from his task to see Milton and the horse coming down his driveway. He grabbed his hat from his head, waved it around like a flag, and threw it on the ground. He then shouted out with enthusiasm, "So, this is how the horse comes back!" To Milton, he said, "How did you know where to bring him?"

Milton answered, "I didn't know the way. The horse knew the way! **I simply kept his attention on the road."**

Following this story, Milton would assure his students: "This is exactly, how to work with anyone. People all know their own way home. **All we need to do is keep their attention on the road."**

Exploring the Process of Holistic Awareness

Metaphors are associative. In a metaphoric story, we are putting together *realizations* as if they were real experiences. There are certain aspects of the whole that may become future instigators—these will emerge holistically, affecting the whole mandala of mind.

For each of us personally, our *life metaphor*, whatever it may be, needs to be explored. Seeing our own life metaphorically gives us room to shift these metaphors and choose them creatively.

We need to see our life as a metaphoric whole experience. This means that our understanding of self emerges like an egg cracking open as the chick steps forth—whole and complete. The experience comes together holistically rather than as a description of a series of events. We experience our life like a mandala, whole and complete, rather than as 'historical bits.'

Telling stories to others gives us power to see our own. We now notice how the sequencing of our logic has become rooted in these metaphors. We turn them into holistic *doorways to creativity* so that mandalic self-discovery emerges. Our self-stories are no longer just nested symbols, but become creative mind-body experiences.

Lining Up Joy in Three Small Steps

Suppose your life was a long line representing all of life's wonderful gifts. On any given day, wherever you happen to be, you can easily traverse your lifeline out even further towards joy.

I have been doing a small exercise daily, which I find valuable, and which I have recommended to others for many years:

- Wherever you happen to be standing, envision a *joy line* stretching out from you to an '*endless horizon of endless joy.*'
- Notice that this amazing luminous line that shines before you is a bright beautiful shade of color (gold, rainbow, white light, or any other color that you love).
- Now think of three joyful things that happened to you so far today… perhaps a first sweet sip of warm tea or a hug from a good friend, a shared joke or a short pause to enjoy the sunshine… or the deep and satisfying reach of your heart towards a dear family member.

- As each thought comes to mind, see yourself taking a tiny symbolic step forward on your joy line, refreshing and expanding your awareness of the day's moments of joy and gratitude.
- One at a time, take each of those three small steps on your line as you remember and re-taste each of your day's joyful moments.
- Remind yourself to continue enjoying your journey to endless joy again tomorrow.
- Notice your joy line as the deepest and most profound journey of your life.

Chapter 2

Identity Explorations, Tribulation, and Discovery

*Consciousness is our Ground of Being!
We do not turn it off.*

—Amit Goswami

The Surfer From Beijing

One spring morning in Beijing, China, I was giving a coaching demonstration for the Coach Training program, **The Art and Science of Coaching**.

Visualize Chen, a strong, dark-haired, black-eyed, young entrepreneur, sitting with me at the front of the room. Chen had a worried expression haunting his handsome face. I had picked him for the demonstration because he had been surprisingly somber and quiet during the program so far.

As we started the process, Chen suddenly began to use the language of a 'choking off' metaphor. He said, "I have a big challenge. I have to do so many things in my life. It is like a huge net and I am caught in it! This is the story of my life." His hand went to his throat, his body slumped, and his breathing stopped as he said this.

I responded with a facial expression and tone of incredulity: "What an interesting story! And you say this is the story of your life? What a story to create for yourself! Do you notice that you keep yourself caught in this metaphor?"

He looked up, puzzled. Now I really had his attention.

I nodded and continued, "People can, in fact, choose a defining metaphor that shapes their lives. Is this the kind of metaphor you want?"

I paused and he looked back thoughtfully. "Really?" he wondered in amazement at the idea.

"Suppose you could find another metaphor for your life?" I asked, smiling. "One you really like and one that would give you more room. What might you choose? What might be a truly useful metaphor for you?"

The group and I watched and waited for a full two minutes as Chen considered this. His eyes first darted down, then he shifted and raised his eyes towards the ceiling.

> Suddenly he brightened, "I know," he said, "Surfing!" His eyes sparkled as he said this.
>
> "How do you see yourself as a surfer?" I asked. "Describe your life as a surfer."
>
> His face lit up and he started to breathe deeply. "I see myself surfing as I did once on a visit to Australia!" he said. His tone became warm as he spoke.
>
> With my encouragement, he began again to review some of the same issues as before, but now he looped in his new imagery as he envisioned himself staying 'relaxed and dancing on the wave,' as an 'inside surfer.'
>
> With further questioning, he next described some "upcoming surfing moments" needed for his work. Now he laughed with pleasure and declared that he was seeing himself staying balanced, having fun, and "floating on the moment," yet still in action.
>
> "I think I can really balance through all this," he declared. "Surfing is my way."
>
> This new movie was clearly sweet for him, and his body softened completely with his revised vision. His tone changed and, with more humor, he said he was now looking forward to the challenge.
>
> I was pleased to see how, in the remaining days of the program, he kidded about surfing and referred to himself as a "surfer dude." On the final day, he reported that an online business meeting had been fabulous; and that he planned to continue surfing through his next challenges.
>
> One more beach bum hit the relaxed wave of his life and transformed it from stress to enjoyment!

Moving Beyond Identity as Tribulation

The metaphors showing *identity as tribulation* are particularly useful tools. These metaphors show people how suffering can open the path to self-discovery, thereby leading to learning and release.

A powerful human development story can illuminate how life transformations occur when a person learns how to move beyond self-delusion. Such a metaphor portrays an identity full of pain caught by inner negativities. Perhaps the person is primarily experiencing the idea of self through *internal evaluation* or comparison with others. Perhaps they experience the idea of self as martyr or as mainly worthy of punishment. Describing this kind of trap assists people to notice similar situations in their own lives.

With our metaphor, we can vividly describe the person's *release from dissociation*. We can detail a scenario that clarifies how that individual breaks through the barrier of an *evaluative belief system*. Such a description provides an especially valuable path for others to follow. The creative insight built into the story opens a door for the listener to move through tribulations (as did the person in the story) and break through their own personal barriers.

The Dynamics

When a person intently listens to a description of their own personal tribulations, they often exhibit a degree of *internal evaluation*. This can take the form of an auditory fixation or a tonal message of comparison. The person speaks to themselves both with negative words and negative tone, repeating an old belief. Their internal commentary may therefore sound like: "*It will always be this way,*" or "*I will always be the outsider,*" or "*This is just the way I ruin everything.*"

Consequently, *dissociation habits* necessarily accompany personal identity taking the form of *self-separation*. The irony is that there is a natural, ingrained instinct to fight for the survival of this dissociated internal identity even if it is a negative barrier to learning and release. People always fight for the survival of whatever they think they are. This continual battle leaves a person little time or energy to experience the richness that can be in their lives.

We are **controlled** by whatever we personally *identify with*, and we **control** anything with which we *dis-identify*. This means that any personal identity viewpoints that ebb and flow (or go *up and down* with other people's evaluations) necessarily become a source of personal *tribulation*. We seem to be at the mercy of the imagined comparison. In this way, people tend to see their *same old story* as their reality.

The most powerful aspect of *identity as tribulation* is that it tends to build a strong *sense of separation* from others. Life lived outside of deep awareness of our fundamental connection to each other is ultimately depressing. A life of carefully held impermeable boundaries, walls, and judgments about oneself is a life of fear, anxiety, internal battles, and continual deep dissociation.

Ongoing self-comparison offers one important and great gift: As humans, we have old, specific *brain habits* to pay attention to *any* pain. The moment pain grabs our attention, we study it and we question it. We want to find a way to move beyond it. Pain interrupts complacency; it destroys the day-by-day melodramas that we may be using as a dream world. Suffering is a great gate to freedom. Stories that show and explain how one can conquer suffering and find release from a painful prison are wonderful gifts.

Gifts of Consciousness

One of the greatest gifts we can give others is to describe even one amazing process of self-discovery, in a story, so that it provides a recipe or roadmap for continued self-exploration. When people experience this transformation in others, they begin to find it in themselves. They begin to wonder about their own potential stretch of vision and imagine their own next level of choice and change.

Your story questions can powerfully begin to lead your listeners into new landscapes of consciousness. With a powerful metaphor, people see the vulnerability of others and of themselves. Any description in a story of *the search for truth* beyond the old self-deceptions, self-judgments, and negative habits calls them to attention.

People start to explore their own *profound inner journey* beyond the dogmas, beliefs, and personages they have taken on as identities. They begin to explore both principle and purpose. They develop new ways for meeting difficulties with grace and power. They begin to stretch their aim and vision to become highly intentioned humans who are able to make strong, realizable contributions to others.

Through the story, the listener begins to really *see* other people making important efforts. They begin to feel each moment of the story deeply. Their true inner awareness begins to open, and through the story they become alive to their own deep questions. A story of a life tribulation is wonderfully useful when it brings this truth to each and all.

Tribulation offers us all, by the most natural path, the gift of greater consciousness. To hear the story of someone discovering his or her path is a true blessing. It encourages us to discover our own path. Metaphoric descriptions open doorways to the listener's own inner realization.

Listening to the story, people truly sense their own personal separation. They begin to let go of all their own areas of small-minded, comfort-zone simplifications. They begin to build their capacity to really listen to others and their needs. They begin to understand the suffering of life and heed it as a path to self-discovery.

When we experience this, we begin to awaken to our deeper realities; and these necessarily bring us to realize our connection to others. Suddenly, we become aware of an inner life that is sweet, true, and beautiful, and we reach out to others to share it.

Margaret's Story:
The Choice to Have Huntington's

When I first met Margaret, I saw an attractive, dark-haired woman with a sad face. She quickly told me her reason for seeking a coach: she had been diagnosed as a carrier of Huntington's disease, a fatal disorder carried through the female gene line. Organized genetically, the etiology of this disease is ominous. The affliction invariably leads to early onset of Alzheimer-like symptoms, slow loss of mental function, and a course towards death within 10 years. To carry the genetic syndrome is a dreary death sentence, with no exceptions. It means that sooner or later the person will begin to develop the symptoms of this disease.

Margaret had only just recently discovered she was a carrier, 'destined to the disease,' just before our first meeting. Her 50-year-old mother had been diagnosed as a carrier only five weeks earlier. At the time of her own diagnosis, just the week before our visit, she was newly pregnant. She had tests run on the amniotic fluid of her fetus, and discovered the fetus was female and also a carrier of Huntington's. Just two months' pregnant, she aborted only three days before seeing me. She currently had one child, a 5-year-old daughter, and had decided, at this point, to keep her daughter untested.

Her main request to me as a coach was to assist her in defining her future. She told me that she felt grief and guilt about the recent abortion. We discussed her aim for a few minutes; and I told her about the idea of a 'timeline,' and suggested it could be a valuable aid to her at this point. She was curious and asked to explore.

In our session together, I had her imagine floating far, far above her whole life 'timeline,' seeing the full continuum and scope of her life, from the beginning of her birth to far distant horizons. I invited her to visualize her life as a bright line down below her. Floating far above her 'life,' she looked down at her visualized line to perceive her inner landscape of possibility. She announced that her timeline 'petered out' about five years ahead of now. She said this made sense to her because her potential child was gone now and, "I feel like I have no future."

I asked her to use her mind's eye and, with that eye, float back along the timeline to the point only seven days before she received the test results and made the choice to abort her baby. I asked her, "Was the decision made with love for the child?" She responded quickly, "It was with love; I felt it was the best thing to do." I asked, "What would you say to this loved one if you could?" She nodded and, with a deep feeling, spoke her sadness, her prayers, and her love for the lost little one. "Now," I suggested, "float back even earlier, before the event occurred. What happens to the guilt? What happens to the grief?"

"It's gone," she replied in a surprised tone. "I feel like a weight has been lifted."

At this point, it looked like a most important task had been completed. Margaret had forgiven herself for her choice, and had sent her unborn child her blessings. Through perceiving her life anew, using the *natural inner logic of her timeline, she had healed her grief. She moved from the razor-edge of the old emotional belief to now appreciating her truth; she had found herself as someone who loved her child and acted from love. She realized this was her 'deeper truth.'*

Then I had a further idea and decided to try it: "From what you've told me, it sounds as if you don't believe you had a choice about getting Huntington's disease," I said. "And it also seems that, with this particular disease, people never know when the onset will happen. People can only guess when the symptoms might begin. They might start early, or very late in life. And that means some people might wait until very late in life for any symptoms to begin, does it not? Right? What if the 'start date' of symptoms is actually where you really do have a major choice? What if this is a choice you can be in charge of?" Margaret pondered this idea.

"If you could, in fact, choose the age to start having Huntington's symptoms: the age when it would be okay for you to have Huntington's, what age might that be?" I asked. "Oh, probably around age 100," she jokingly replied.

*"Interesting," I responded. "Are you willing to truly plan it that way? Your deeper intuitive mind is incredibly capable. It beats your heart for you, breathes for you, and heals illness. Perhaps you will get Huntington's someday, but only your unconscious mind can decide exactly when. If you ask it, do you think it could answer your request to plan the onset of this disease **appropriately** for you? Could you request that you wait until you are 100 years old to begin it?*

She immediately brightened as she considered this idea. "I think so," she said slowly. She was immediately cheered, and a sparkle came back into her eye. I assisted her as she 'asked inwardly,' and felt a 'positive' response. "Well, that settles that!" she said.

Suddenly she remembered that her timeline 'disappeared' only five years in future. I pointed out that she was the editor of her inner map.

"Do you want to stretch out your line then?" I asked. "Just notice how rubbery a timeline is. Anyone can lengthen his or her timeline by 'just doing it!' In your mind's eye, you can reach down, grab one end of

> it, and pull it out like elastic, all the way to age 100! Watch it lengthen as you do so," I said, pointing to a hypothetical visual image. She nodded, and seemed very surprised at her inner result: she could now comfortably visualize a long, strong, glowing line "out to one hundred." To make it stay, she fastened it inwardly with a vision of strong Velcro.
>
> Before she left my office, she spoke one more time to her lost unborn child: "I will take care of you," she said. "I'll take you through life with me. I love you."
>
> She smiled when she left, and said she was 'totally complete.' This was our only coaching session. No more was wanted for her purpose. Since then, I met her several times in the city where she and her family moved. She looks and sounds well.

A Pilgrim In The World

Through a story, we can *see* a person as he or she begins to experience a fundamental and often humbling connection to each and every person around him or her. We see how this may start out as bewildering, but then *watch and listen* as the experience described in the story opens the person's evolution towards into a deeper level of self-recognition and warm regard for others.

What does such a story provide? Often, we see a journey evolve from pride to despair into *presence*. Our belief in *offended entitlement* gets shattered. Like the person in the story, we lose self-importance.

This is a great gift of all tribulation. Leaving behind self-importance allows us the freedom to become a true explorer of life. We leave the pompous relics of self-conceit and step forth, willing to see others afresh. Emotions shift to the experience of connection, relaxation, enjoyment, certainty, and love.

Now we can be simple pilgrims on the path of self-discovery. Our story begins anew.

Chapter 3

Seeding Metaphoric Landscapes

You want to know of Death?
Well, I shall save my breath.
When you really know Life, why then
We'll talk of Death again.

—Confucius

Scripted Emotions = Previously Recorded Conclusions

Most humans live in an inner world filled with *scripted emotions*, which are merely *previously recorded conclusions* and microscopic metaphors of entangled and often contradictory self-expectations.

These *previously scripted emotions* are just sad old *mind-movies* about self-importance, self-dissociation, self-pity, and self-deception. Most of these memories are simply boring old repetitive laments. We call them *ego-organizing metaphors* because when examined they magnify *associative self-focus* as well as *self-judgment*.

Throughout the world's cultures, scripted emotions of this type are currently more the norm than not. Yet these emotional scripts or *misery landscapes* are often akin to barren and windswept desert plains—stripped of richness and growth.

Example: An elderly married couple had been together for 60 years. The wife was on her deathbed while the husband reassured her that he loved her: "*Throughout our marriage, I always made sure to eat the crusts of the bread so you didn't have to,*" he said. "*And I always wanted them!*" she replied.

What does it mean if, for 60 years, we refrain from telling our partner what we want? It means that, for 60 years, we listen to an inner lament. We are only hearing our own, stoical, rule-bound self-scripts: "I have to, need to, or must..."

The example of the old couple is just one tiny example. Often we find these stories to be enlarged, dissociated, identity metaphors—barren of all joy or hope. "*I will never have love in my life because...*" (... And the violins in our mind take up their refrain.)

Negative thoughts go around in a vicious circle—one big never-ending loop—starting with comparative and negative internal commentary and leading right back to the same old negative feelings. People get into a state of depression that leads to the beginning of the sad, old scripted story all over again.

Ask these questions when you encounter negative repetitive emotions:
- Can the context of this be perceived?
- Is this person or team lost from context awareness?
- Are they still lost inside the story emotionally?

- Do they really believe their own sad tale?
- Can they learn to step from the story they tell themselves and enter the viewpoint and experience of others?

A strong consciousness metaphor accomplishes three main things:

1) It allows people to move away from their own joyless old story and view it from a much richer emotional perspective that carries a positive outcome. They may see a resemblance to themselves in the main character of the story. They begin to view the scenario from an observer or coach perspective.

2) It rebuilds a context of truth telling and self-awareness for the listener. It disables the listener's own old story. When hearing a story of self-realization, the listener experiences a release from this old repetitive identity. This changes everything, allowing their personal barren wasteland to flourish and once again produce new growth.

3) It opens positive emotions, particularly laughter. This allows the person to experience a joyful release so that they now laugh at their old habits, roles, and rules that they once believed were a depressing cross to bear. They find they are able to enjoy the idea of breaking the habit.

The joy of laughter opens wide the doorway to self-realization. The process happens spontaneously and organically. Laughter breaks down the barriers of the mind and body to let in change and let out sad old prophesies. There is a wonderful physical expansion of one's entire being when we laugh.

Beyond the Death Mask

Scripted emotions preordain that we do not ask for what we want and need. They are like small computer programs that work on their own. Through scripted emotions, it is easy to fall prey to the *great fear gremlins*:

- fear of dreaming
- fear of failure
- fear of offending people
- fear of conflict

Much of scripted emotion is entirely mechanical. It's an automatic replay of an inner voice that gets fired up without any rational reason.

Example: An argument flares up between a couple not for any current reason, but simply from the *tonal inner recordings* of an old quarrel being replayed again and again in the mind. The angry tones of a previous nasty disagreement with a mate become a *vocal tape-recording* replayed and reheard inwardly. One or two years later, that tone and perhaps a few of the same words in a totally different context will allow the old, angry feelings about a partner to resurface. Through a meaningless repetition of an ancient recording now amplified, the old feelings get moved to the present and the couple finds themselves once again fighting… *but actually fighting the same old fight they've had the previous year!* Inner strings are pulled and the puppets move into a meaningless dance.

Through strong metaphorical images, we assist our listeners to find the silent place where they can hear the beautiful truths of someone in a similar situation and observe their best moments and outcomes.

It bears repeating that the passive constricted whisperings and the old pictures and flat recordings that lead to *scripted emotions* are mostly on a circular loop which amplifies them. People listen again and again to the same voices expressing the same concerns. Round and round the inner discussion goes.

If they pay attention, they will notice that these voices are sometimes comparing their self to others, with negative internal commentary. What are the dynamics of this? Often the inner voice uses self-identifications that are not effective to the development of our life experience as a whole. The internal voice says, "*I am,*" as in "*I am this kind of person…*" when, in actual fact, that isn't who we are at all. It may speak falsehoods in the form of vast generalizations, as in "*I will never…*" This quickly leads to feelings of separation and loss.

Internal images connected to scripted emotions have been studied and found to have some interesting qualities.

- They are usually flat pictures devoid of color.
- They have us see our self-image as smaller than others… or larger.
- They may see the self as controlled by others.

- They associate the self with only one position, one viewpoint, and one emotional tone.
- They find the self in a pale inner landscape of dissociation—a dream world of death.
- Often the visual image has come to a dead stop... A snapshot has been created of the most negative part... That triggers the internal commentary.

What happens when these negative visuals become ingrained habits for people? They find themselves with black and white thoughts, narrowed focus, and little capacity to notice self-development.

All inner stoppages for self or others are reflected by recorded *inner judgments*, which may be experienced as immediate conclusions of alarm. After a negative outcome, an inner voice might conclude: "*This failed and it means something is wrong.*" Usually it means something is wrong with **you** (you are inadequate, ineffective, or blameworthy in some way).

The inner story may express causes and effects of personal survival that are lies. For example, it tells us that certain behaviors or beliefs will harm us or protect us. It tells us that, in fact, we are *not* going to survive; there is no way to get out of here alive! It tells us that life will go on without us, pass us by, and we are stuck with the old, sad story.

These types of conclusions disconnect people from their real lives. They take up all the inner space and don't allow any room for new learning, new connections, and new life experiences. They discourage curiosity. They reduce the chance that the person will try something experiential and adventurous.

Opening Pathways With Stories of Self-Realization

Through storytelling, you can help lead someone to open and find a path to his or her inner awareness. This means they regain hope for self-renewal. How do you help them move beyond their scripted emotions?

Stories of self-realization offer a descriptive pathway that shows detailed examples of how one can manifest power, energy, and purpose. Through the story, people begin to realize the inner light of consciousness itself. Through your story, you assist someone to walk along the trail of inner awareness with you, to find a peaceful moment. The doorway to inner awareness is always available. The rich inner growth of awareness can again be spoken about.

What happens when, in your story, you describe a process wherein someone moves beyond the constant inner tape recordings to the spacious quiet that goes with the promise of new beginnings? You show your listener a way to become curious about what will take him or her beyond their own emotional inner dialogue, with stories of others who have done the same thing, shifting to renewal. The *metaphoric vision* aids people to reconnect to their own inner reach for positive possibilities. It becomes immediately possible for them to find their own deeper truth.

If we intently observe, we can see beyond any old *death mask* to a genuinely live person. That person will lift his or her eyes when we look at them. That person's true being will start to peek out when we connect. Then, that person will shyly step forward, and a different conversation can take place—both inwardly and outwardly.

The Russian Radio

The Russian Radio story that follows is designed to raise curiosity about internal dialogue, the 'carrier' of the virus of negative emotions.

When I first started teaching courses in Russia in 1989, just after Glasnost, I would often find myself in a Soviet-era countryside health resort, which offered a rural setting for my program. When I opened the door to my hotel room, I would typically be greeted by blaring Russian voices from a tiny wall radio. These resorts and their wall radios were often identical, city-to-city.

The first thing that I would do after setting down my luggage would be to hunt for the wall radio, and turn it off. But, normally I would find only a small finger device, built into the wall, with only one tiny knob for volume. They were built so that the volume could only go up or down, but not off! Even when the volume switch was turned down all the way, a tiny sound could still be heard.

> *The Russian radio would go off at midnight with an anthem, and would start again at 6:00 a.m. I would be in my morning meditation and the barely discernable voice would suddenly appear again. This tiny, scratchy sound would continually remain present in the recesses of the room.*
>
> *Think about this. Isn't this exactly like your own 'internal dialogue' system? We all have a variety of voices, always available to be heard, if you listen for them. If we pay attention, we notice that the messages are largely repetitive. They may also be emotional and negative, creating mindsets and moods. How will you begin to **widen your attention** to move beyond the random message system? Hear the Russian radio? Now, **widen your attention**.*

Creating Inner Gardens Using Open-Ended Questions

How do we create a growing garden of awareness through metaphor? One way to reseed the barren field is to ask rich open-ended questions throughout your story. Open-ended questions are questions designed to help people add detail and dimensions to their perceptions. They stir the imagination and spark the fires of growth. All humans are innately mystics and attracted to grace and beauty. A story of self-realization opens everyone's heart.

We ask questions in the context of the story in the same way a person must ask them in a powerful coaching session. Through our questions, we show linkages between our wider positive questions and positive growth. We add visions of decision making, life energy, and truthful renewal. We show values blooming in a life and encourage people to realize the potential of their own *inner garden of growth*.

Open-ended questions are a tool that coaches can use to assist the listener to search for new levels of coherency. By asking strong questions, we are inviting our listeners to renew their inner self-expression and positive vision. These open-ended questions send our listeners on a search for self-knowledge. Open-ended questions in a story are questions that are designed to help people add detail and dimensions to their perceptions.

Notice that the functions of open-ended questions are threefold:

1) **Open-ended questions** respond respectfully to a person's experience just as the person describes it, without confusion with anyone else's ideas.

2) **Open-ended questions** acknowledge aspects of the person's perception or experience that may be out of the person's conscious awareness, yet available through questions.

3) **Open-ended questions** are a tool that all of us can use to assist others to explore the symbols and metaphors that make up their *mind maps* and *mental landscapes*, sending people on an inward search for self-knowledge.

When you ask people strong open-ended questions, people will search inwardly, beyond everyday conscious-mind thinking, moving through their entire experience to come up with their own answers!

Marie and the Shock Treatments

An example of 'decisive mind change' happened one day, many years ago, with a client named Marie. In our first, short, information-gathering session, Marie and I had discussed her dream to have a "normal life." I discovered that she believed that she was a profoundly broken person. I looked at the pretty, curly-headed, intelligent and humorous 20-year-old girl, feeling inwardly puzzled as she told me her story: "In the last four years, I have had 160 shock treatments," she reported.

Around age 16, she had started fighting occasionally with her mother over small things. (Very normal behavior for a teenager beginning to assert her independence, I thought.) But, for Marie, this desire to assert herself met her own strong self-disapproval. In inner conflict, she asked her mother to allow her to see a psychiatrist.

A thought flashed by me of how similar she was to me at age 15. As a teen, I had run away from home; and later visited a psychiatrist for several self-exploration sessions. (We mostly just sat there, as I recall, and I was quite disappointed.)

What Marie told me amazed me. Her mother's random choice of psychiatrists had clearly proved to be catastrophic. In their first session, the psychiatrist decided that Marie needed shock treatments. He hospitalized her immediately, and delivered a series of 16 'treatments.'

She described how, when she returned from the hospital, her fearful family treated her like a very sick patient. With memory loss from the treatments, she could no longer go to school; and she stayed passively at home being assisted by her concerned parents.

Marie continued with her story. She described the beginnings of a new habit, the 'shock treatment habit.' Marie was the center of concern in her home, as she gradually regained her memory. Some irritation with her parents' overprotection began to appear. A crazy cycle started. Time after time, year after year, she ordered a taxi, drove back to the state hospital, phoned her psychiatrist, and demanded more shock treatments; and he gave them to her.

Now, 160 shock treatments and four years later, Marie sat in my office pleading for a normal life. "It almost sounds like you developed a shock treatment addiction," I mused upon hearing her story. "Trying new things is normal for young people," I said, "but this was a difficult one, wasn't it?"

"It meant I never finished school," she said. "I never got to learn."

"Well, you're learning now," I said. "Your responses to the situation seem very real, accurate, and authentic to yourself. You tell me you want a normal life?" Marie nodded. "Tell me, then, what is your vision? Is this aim for a normal life important enough for you that you will do what it takes to get it?"

With this, Marie talked about her hopes and dreams. I encouraged her to continue. She talked about a chance to date, like others her age. She discussed a chance to dance and have fun, and even a chance to marry and have a family. She spoke about her values: She talked about more education and what kind of a student she wanted to be. She described what kind of a mother she wanted to be. I encouraged her. "So, you have strong values and hopes," I noted. *How can you begin to make them real now? What will be your own pathway into life?*

Relaxed and exploratory, Marie now followed her curiosity about her old fears. I asked her what instigated them? She mused, wandered back through her life with curiosity, and suddenly remembered a decision she made as a child to never 'cause' her mother to get upset. She specifically remembered a time when she was only a small girl, housebound for a month with three older sisters, during a severe winter storm. They lived far in the country and off the school bus route. Her mother had attempted to home-school the four daughters, but came often to frustration as the girls laughed and played instead of studying. Several times she spoke angrily to them, "You never behave. You make me totally tired out! I can't manage you at all," she said. "I am going crazy trying to take care of you."

Her story continued. One day, her mother left home and stayed in a hospital for one month, because of a breakdown. Marie was horrified, and felt that she had personally caused her mother to have problems. She vowed that if her mother came home, she would never cause her trouble again.

As Marie related the story, I listened carefully. "So, for you at that time, it seemed as though you actually caused your mother's illness?" I asked, with an incredulous tone. *A young girl can easily become mistaken, and doesn't understand that one person cannot cause illness in another. What if that child had discovered, instead, how each person is completely in charge of his or her own inner state? What if she had learned that only we can be in charge of our own inner world and cause our own feelings, and that other people own their own? What if she learned that no one can cause another person to have any emotional problem? That our feelings always belong to ourselves?*

She wondered openly as I became curious about her learning. "I guess I always knew that," she said. "At least, I do know it now: no one can 'make' another person tired or upset. We always have our own results, don't we? I was small. I just didn't understand."

> "Hey, hey, Marie," I said. "Being self-responsible means a lot, and I'm glad to hear you notice that you can decide for yourself. Otherwise, we are all robots!"
>
> Then she giggled for a moment. "It's rather funny, really," she said, "It is rather hilarious when you think about it! I will never do that again! What a mistake!" She started to giggle a little more, and then to laugh deeply. "It's really funny," she said. Holding her sides, she laughed more and more. Sliding off her chair onto the carpet, she rolled about for a moment, kicking her feet with hilarity and holding her sides. For about two minutes, she howled with laughter as I watched in surprise. Then she got up, calmly dusted herself off, and said emphatically: "Well, I don't **ever** have to do that again!"
>
> And she didn't. Twenty years later, I saw her occasionally when I dropped into the interesting specialty shop she owned in my city. She used her one coaching session to stand firmly in her key decision to renew her life on her own terms.

Listening to Inner Knowledge

In the story, we both ask and *listen* as we ask. Our listeners will observe and also learn from the mere fact that we are listening. As we ask open-ended questions, we demonstrate the process of listening carefully to our *own inner* knowledge. We also ask open-ended questions and demonstrate the process of listening carefully to others, even as we continue to tell our stories.

We show the process of *pondering* and *wondering* and, in doing so, we demonstrate the inner awareness that goes with pondering. As with the shift in breathing for a kayaker listening to and matching the rhythm of the paddle, we now demonstrate the shift in how we listen appreciatively to *our inner awareness* throughout the story. Our listeners start to follow and match as well.

These listening and pondering attitudes can be examined in the self-discovery process in your story. You can describe them in the step-by-steps of the story's unfolding. Developed through the metaphor, they lead to your listeners pondering, exploring, and listening to their own inner questions.

These shifts are wonderful to describe in an unfolding metaphor; they show the power of a *tipping point change*. A person or group might live from the belief: *"If I take care of my needs, I won't be valued."* A story can be told that shows a reversal of this so that another stronger understanding of true value can emerge. Or, *"I'm not liked because I don't act confident enough!"* In the story, we watch a person grow and develop, learning how to find inner certainty. The listeners ponder and release the old belief.

Example: In Marie's story, her belief that *"I must keep my mother safe from anger,"* was dissolved as she moved to reflection and self-discovery. *"I will never do that again"* is her triumphant release—a great punch line! Her story assists others pondering renewal and commitment to find their own self-discovery pathway.

In designing your story, take time to ask yourself:
- **Where** do people dissociate?
- **Where** do they forget what is truly important to them?
- **How** do they dissociate?
- **How** can they discover a way to refocus and stay on track?
- **How** do they discover it and claim it with power and purpose?
- **What** is their larger purpose?

As you design your story, you can now show the release and refocus on inner self-discovery that will trigger the new growth for your listeners. One metaphor can accomplish a lot. The newly seeded questions grow. The old landscapes now flower with renewal.

Red-Haired Men

What is a phobia? To anyone on the outside, a phobia seems completely irrational. Yet, to the afflicted person, the fears are strong and compelling.

Visit an episode many years ago. A conversation between a psychologist and an elegant female lawyer offers us insight. Picture the scene. The lawyer revealing her phobia, with some embarrassment, to her counselor: "I cannot stand red-haired men!" she says. "I know it sounds crazy but I don't trust them at all. They are dangerous. The worst part is that next week our new organizational chief will start in our city office. He is arriving from Toronto and will be my boss." "And," she added with a choke, "he has flaming red hair. I don't know him, but I have seen his picture. I am afraid I will have to quit. It's a big challenge."

See, in your mind's eye, this young and attractive woman seriously discussing her dismal options. "What is it about red-haired men?" the psychologist inquired. "Don't try to change my mind," she replied stiffly. "Basically, they are all jerks."

"Amazing," the psychologist said. "So, for you, at this point, it seems like there is no hope of keeping your job in the legal firm?" She made a face, shivered, and nodded, looking sad.

There are many ways to work with phobias, but the psychologist was curious because the woman was so seriously concerned. How do we make our fears so real when they are phantoms?

The psychologist asked her to go into her memory bank for a moment, and allow her mind to wander way back to recall the first time she had created the belief that red-haired men were dangerous. "It is okay to observe again for a moment," offered the psychologist. "What do you find?"

She bit her lip. "I do recall it," she said. "I'm two years old, playing catch with my brother with a big beach ball. We are on the front lawn, which slopes towards the street. I miss the ball and it slowly rolls *down the lawn, over the curb, and into the road. There are no cars in the cul-de-sac so I follow the ball to retrieve it. Suddenly, a milk truck turns into the road, going very fast. I am bending over to get the ball and the milk truck screeches to a halt. It is scary! Out gets a tall guy with bright red hair and, with angry hands, he picks me up and puts me on the curb. 'Don't you ever do that again, little girl,' he says in a strong tone."*

That was the incident that produced a lifetime of difficult situations. What we put our attention on, we get more of. Not surprisingly, all the red-haired men after this first one fell into the same category... difficult and possibly dangerous.

It did not take long for the counselor to reverse her client's phobia. The fear was quickly vanquished and, with some further work, the lawyer dismissed her conclusion about all red-haired men as perhaps 'an overstatement.' "*I am willing to give the new office chief a chance. Perhaps it was all a coincidence!*" *she said. Cheerful, she left the counselor's office.*

A phobia is not difficult to work with: this was a single-session event. For this client, the discovery that she saw people through her expectations was the big result. She stayed with her law firm, but also began to test her own perceptions.

After one more session, every red-haired man in her life was given a reprieve. For her, just to realize that she created her own results jolted her awake to her blind spots; it started new learnings that continued to deepen. The discovery was highly relevant to the next steps in her growth as a person.

Chapter 4

Why Do Humans Suffer?

*There is a crack in everything.
That's how the light gets in!*

—Leonard Cohen

Step Beyond Metaphoric Suffering to Enlightened Awareness

Did you ever consider that most suffering starts with a 'negative metaphor' that people repeat to themselves?

Suffering can be defined as "**not being with**," or "a pain about a pain." In other words, we are talking about *metaphoric pain* we produce giving us an experience of helplessness and anxiety.

Often this is a story that disconnects us from the future. Suffering is inherent in the *belief* that we do not have a real connection to a future. When we pity ourselves, through our inner story, we tell ourselves that we won't get *to have* the future that we want—**then** we suffer.

Ideas about time, as in the phrase: "…. *my short lifetime*," are often found in this type of suffering. The root of the word time comes from "*indefinite frame of continuous duration*" or "*something that does not continue*" or "*something that is cut off.*" We make ourselves small with the idea of *personal time as limitation*. The usual visualization of time is an hourglass—the '*egg timer of life and rebirth.*' It's easy to visualize sand running through an hourglass and our sand running out.

Notice that to others, our metaphors can shift this life script. We can assist people to rebuild their inner connection to a future by showing the potency of life rediscovery through our story.

Again, it is like the 'hourglass.' We need only to turn our '*timer*' upside down to experience rebirth. There is an old saying: "… *turning over a new leaf.*" We are all perfectly capable of simply reaching out and flipping that hourglass on its head, especially regarding our life complaints where we focused on old opportunities now gone.

People always have a connection to a future, but it is not and cannot be *personal*! The idea of *personal time* is an illusion! It is a private hope destined to be disappointed, simply through definition. We move 'our future' forward when we show how one person's life opens up another's. We 'turn over our timer' to a wider vision, and we experience rebirth. Our true life and future is like passing the baton is for the relay runner. We are all on humanity's team.

Suffering results from the attempt to avoid '**not being**.' *Dissociation* is what we do when we come across something that we feel is unbearable. *Suffering*, as dissociation, means that when something is '*too terrible to be with*,' we are '*not with it*.' Paradoxically, **when we are '*not with it*,' we are not even aware that we are '*not with it*'**! So, simply put: "*We are not with it that we are not with it.*" We experience '***not being***' to avoid not *being*. This is truly ironic. Pity the small idea of time as limitation. In what wider vision do you find yourself okay? Truly **being** okay, fulfilled and free, on humanity's team? When we tell stories that connect people to this wider vision, time as limitation falls away! One has only to reach out and flip over the *timer* to begin a new beginning!

This can provide wonderful motivation for you, the metaphor developer. Move people into their true lives with stories that empower their wider vision of life for all. Time-suffering beliefs provide stockpiles of theories that shrivel both motivation and joy. People imagine a future in which they see the '*others*' of their world enjoying life, feasting, playing, and getting rewards. This is a fabulous future they feel they do not share. The pictures in their imagination of the fabulous future include people they compare themselves to. They view '*these lucky ones*' as people enjoying their lives, but envision that they (themselves) are not *with* them!

We tell stories that shatter this self-deception. We whisper through our metaphor:

> *Turn over your hourglass!*
> *Stand your suffering on its head!*
> *Turn over your future to enlightened awareness.*

What do stories that connect to enlightened awareness show us?

- They show us a timelessness of learning that moves people into wider awareness.
- They show us people learning how to connect to inner trust and deep faith in life.
- They show us renewal and rebirth.

Are you interested in finding and developing some stories that do this?

The Drunkard From Chelyabinsk

Let me tell you about an event which occurred in Chelyabinsk, Russia, in the early 1990s. I once worked with a thin, disheveled, young alcoholic during a training demonstration that was part of an addictions program for psychologists. This man, Sergei, who was experiencing severe health issues including liver damage, hoped to convince himself to quit drinking… immediately. During our conversation, he found a dominant internal objection that stopped all forward movement: "If I stop drinking, I'll lose all my friends!" he said chokingly, in a trembling voice. His body slumped and he briefly stopped breathing.

After his reaction, I asked: "Is it possible that you could stop drinking and you **won't** lose all your friends?" As he considered this, I continued: "What if you **don't** quit drinking? Might you lose all your friends anyway?"

These simple questions produced a major shift for Sergei, because he had never really considered the larger field of possibilities before. He had always placed himself in mental turmoil by reacting emotionally to his first and strongest inner objection.

I watched Sergei's expression change as he considered these contradictory options; he began to think clearly about what he truly wanted. That day, Sergei became serious about his choices, and eventually made the critical and major changes that ended his addiction and recharged his life.

In Your Secret Heart: A Meditation

In everyone's *secret heart*, there is a doorway to self-awareness, like a garden gate. For fun, physicalize this vision.

Go to that place in the core of your being, the gate to your secret heart. Open the latch and go through the door into your own secret garden of inner being. In your mind, look around you.

- What is your inner garden of self-awareness like?
- Be there and just breathe for a moment!
- Sense the space and notice the surroundings. Notice the qualities.
- What is the inner *view* like?
- What does this inner space *feel* like?
- What do you enjoy here?
- What are the *tastes, smells, and touche*s like?
- Are there any *sounds* or is there *silence*?

Be there and just breathe it all in. Relax inside your place of self-awareness.

The Story of Victor Frankl

*Have you heard of Victor Frankl, the great Second World War author who wrote the book, "Man's Search for Meaning"? During four years in a concentration camp, he made a decision to make his suffering meaningful. He promised himself to find a way for his years of death camp experience to become a value 'container' that could contribute to others. And he determined to strongly declare even **that** possibility while he was experiencing 'the worst.'*

Let me detail the story. Picture a two-acre, electric barbed wire enclosure with small cabins in the middle. Picture the guards who watched, armed with submachine guns, ready to kill anyone who approached the fence. Suicide was easy.

*This was the context where Victor Frankl asked himself, "How can I find meaning… even here?" He powerfully spoke his aim to the other inmates of the prison camp until he created an inner circle, a small group of men who all shared the same intent. They promised each other that, simply through intent, the death camp experience would **dissolve** and **evolve** into something of value for their own lives* *and for others around them. They started declaring that they would find a way to make the experience produce something meaningful not only for themselves but for all humanity.*

Victor promised to assist others around him with this task and, day-by-day and week-by-week, he and the others did exactly that. He and the other men would gather at night in a circle talking to any suicidal person amongst them. With each one, they would ask: What could invigorate the will to live, even there in the midst of horror and despair? They asked this question again and again.

For each person, with the support of the others, they would eventually discover this person's key life purpose. Then they would help this person to accept this as a contract to keep living no matter how terrible the life.

For one man, a doctor, it was a discovery of medical knowledge that he could eventually contribute to others. For another, it was a book of poetry. For a third, it was a slight chance that his young daughter was alive somewhere and would need him after the war. For a fourth, it was a novel he knew he wanted to write.

After sitting in the circle talking about their vision and reinventing the purpose of their lives, they would make a joint promise. Together, day-by-day, they used this to encourage each other to survive even another day no matter what. They declared a purpose, and the declaration became the space of their life. They developed the capacity to do what they agreed.

Following that powerful choice, and the experience of value that he committed to, the 'worst situation' became a doorway to Frankl's own awakened mind. His powerful book about this, "Man's Search for Meaning," has assisted millions.

The Process of Creating Purpose

Transformational awareness results from expanding perception. We assist by linking values with visual imagery through genuine *declarations of renewal*. Repeating declarations, purpose statements, reframes, or 'punch lines' produces true evocative power. These statements and declarations—often one-liners—are *telling phrases* yielding *principles* that have onomatopoeia power, the ring of congruence.

Onomatopoeia means that the word sounds like the sound associated with it. The principle rings forth and sticks in our brain, bringing the 'value feeling' with it!

Example: "*Plop, plop, fizz, fizz,* oh what a relief it is."
—Alka-Seltzer jingle, USA.

A key aim with a strong story is to assist the listener to create transformational questions! People may never consciously ask: "How is *this* story *my* story?" Yet, they begin to consider the 'life questions' inside the story *as if they were their own*. In this way, they quickly start expanding the parameters of their own inner awareness.

The Life of David Rigmore

How can you keep the human spirit alive in a 1-by-2-meter cell for 12 years, alone in the dark and isolated, with little food? David's story, next, shows the way for all of us to learn the art of persistent commitment, purpose, and vision, despite all obstacles.

Let me tell you the amazing and remarkable story of David Rigmore. I was lucky to be part of a small group listening to his story one winter evening in Seattle 15 years ago. What was David's tale? See a tall and scraggly 70-year-old man with big eyes and a wide grin, relating the story that follows.

As an eager young art student in the 1950s, David fell in love with ancient Chinese ceramics and determined to go to China to study them. There, he got caught up in the huge revolutionary war leading to the Communist regime. His parents in Seattle pleaded with him: "Come home David. Come home!" But, he was determined to stay and, after the Communists took power, he became an 'Art Guide,' taking visitors on tours to see great Chinese works of art. He learned the language, married a Chinese woman, and had two children. Enjoying his life, he continued to study his passion, Chinese ceramics. Despite many ups and downs to come, and his parents' pleas, he stayed for 12 years and raised his children there.

Then came the terrible era of the 'Gang of Four.' All intellectuals and educated people in the major cities were sent to the countryside, and some were imprisoned. David was one of them. One morning, he was taken to prison, and to the cell that became his home for 12 years.

Consider waking up in the morning as David: You are in the pitch-black darkness with only a tiny thread of light at the bottom of the heavy iron door. The door has a tiny double opening at the top for passing in the one meal you will receive that day, watery soup and bread. The room has only a straw mat and two pails, one with drinkable water. How would you keep your hope, your energy, your intelligence, and your life commitment in this place? For 12 years?

David gave every day his purpose and focus. His purpose was to stay alive, fully functioning, and, if possible, to return to his family. Each day, he made an inner promise **to create the privilege of being alive**. *As he explained it: "I needed to keep my energy alive; this included my physical energy, my emotional energy, my mental capacity, and my vision. I needed to keep my inner flame burning, my creative focus, and my capacity for love!"*

How did he do it? For 12 years, in the dark? Getting up each morning, he would vision his day as life's great gift. He said, "If I had no life at all, then this simple life I do have is truly a great opportunity."

Each morning, he began to recreate his physical energy. Making space for three paces down his cell and three paces back, he would walk for hours. He would envision one of the trails he loved as a youth, or a winding country road in France.

Following forest, and an unfolding vision, he would imagine a brilliant sunny day and feel the sunshine on his skin. He would see rolling green hills and fill in details: occasional villages, farms, hay-fragrant barns with flowers, and children playing. Imagining rural France, he would smell the warm French air, feel the breezes blow in his hair, and sense the strength in his muscles. At each moment he remembered, he would feel gratitude: **creating the privilege of being alive, one holy day at a time**.

He said his walks gave him great pleasure and heightened his spirits: "I would have some fun," he said. "Imagine setting down for lunch on a grassy field, and chewing crusty French bread and strong cheese. Or, imagine finding yourself in the long grass, with ladybugs and buzzing with grasshoppers. Then imagine holding sugar in your hand till a grasshopper lands on your palm. Imagine watching it slowly chewing the sugar with large jaws, mandibles moving, then suddenly flying up and away with a buzz."

In the afternoon, he would play chess with himself, using 'chess pieces' made of bread. "I would sit and carefully play one side only. I would make my move. Then, moving across carefully, I would switch and play the other side," he said. "Sometimes I would be so hungry. I would want to eat the chess pieces." Later, he would sing and create songs. He would create poems and prayers, learn them, and memorize them.

Finally, in late afternoon, the one fateful hour approached when he would actually have a chance to talk with a human being: the guard who brought his single meal once per day. He would await this person eagerly, hoping and planning for communication. At last would come the fateful moment, to open the small frame at the top of his door and briefly view the face of the teenage guard bringing his meal.

He described how he would talk casually: "How's it going for you today?" He was always hoping for a moment of real communication, real contact. If the guard paused, as would happen once every six months, he would chat about the weather, work, anything that a young Chinese guard might discuss, hoping to create a friendship. Once in a long while, someone would stop for a moment and really discuss the world outside the heavy iron door: a brief contact that he would mentally replay, and enjoy, in the days that followed. One day in the life, 12 years of these days, and always, each morning, **creating the privilege of being alive**. Life, hope, and another day alive.

What is the conclusion of this story? What brought David to the small, startled group in Seattle where I found myself listening and pondering in amazement?

> *David described it simply. One day, with no expectation, a man came and unlocked all of the doors in his cellblock. "You are free to go," he said to the bewildered prisoners, leading them to the door. "Get out of here."*
>
> *Suddenly, David found himself in the bright sunlight of Beijing, wandering through streets full of people. He had no money or food. He went on a three-day walk, searching for his wife and children, and eventually finding them.*
>
> *His family in the United States, upon hearing he was alive, immediately wired him money: "Come home, David, come home!" This time, with wife and family, he honored their request.*
>
> *Again, looking at the peaceful warm person in front of me, I saw someone still intent on honoring the privilege of being alive. What did David continue to do for his living, someone asked. "Well," he said laughing. "What I like best is taking people on art tours in China."*
> **Create the privilege of being alive!**

The Hero's Journey

The story of David Rigmore describes a Hero's Journey. The Hero's Journey is a genre of story about a person with a strong purpose meeting and moving through life's challenges. Many of the stories in this book are Hero's Journeys.

The key qualities you will find in such stories:
- They clearly depict the unfolding of the Hero's Journey—the development of a person who stretches beyond his or her own expectations and limits, both in engaging his or her full life and engaging fully with others.
- They show glimpses of key points in that person's development as he or she emerges as a person of character, integrity, self-knowledge, and trust.
- They are often are about a warrior, a cultural creative, a champion, or a leader.

- They demonstrate making powerful commitments in the face of inner and outer hardships; we hear about the person's challenges and the unfolding learning.

Usually, we follow the hero as he or she goes through a compelling progression of difficulties that unfolds as specific steps in his or her self-discovery. We explore these steps in the unfolding story.

The hero is challenged:

First, the hero starts out being thrust into a challenge. Life moves him or her into the face of a challenge. The hero is surprised or challenged in such a way that they feel they must begin to learn and grow. The universe offers a unique job or quest, and our hero accepts the opportunity. Good examples can be seen in all of the world's great literature: Homer's *Odyssey*; biblical figures such as Abraham or David; those found in twentieth-century popular literature such as Tolkien's *Lord of the Rings* trilogy; and C. S. Lewis's *Chronicles of Narnia*. All these show the hero being propelled into the *fire of action*—whether he or she wants it or not.

The hero commits:

At the start of the journey, further challenges appear. The person takes a stand, saying, "*I will do it!*" and makes a *declaration of commitment*. They begin to undergo inner shifts, developing courage, resilience, tenacity, and other characteristics of leadership and strength. Gradually, they solidify this commitment and inevitably cross an internal threshold. The individual gradually moves into clarity and certainty of his or her capacities.

The hero is tested and asks for help:

Next, overwhelming challenges present themselves. Sorely tested, the person learns to ask for help. He or she seeks or stumbles across guardians and helpers who assist when he or she asks. As they request assistance, they find that others answer the call. Our hero learns inner and outer trust, even in the face of adversity.

The hero finds advisors:

Whether these are inner or outer fears, the challenges at first may seem to be evil. The hero learns to work with the difficulties, eventually transforming them into valuable resources that can be used in his or her quest.

The hero develops resources:

In meeting these extraordinary challenges, the hero accesses resources and develops special skills and tools. They discover their own strengths and acquire mastery. Our hero takes ownership and brings their resources back to assist others.

The return home:

The story ends with a genuine form of expansive celebration. The hero returns home and everyone reunites and celebrates. The hero has moved past inner and outer challenges, has grown and developed on many levels and, as a result, brings back a true contribution to others.

The result:

Everyone feels happy but, more than that, they can partake in the growth and development that the hero has opened to all.

Chapter 5

Transforming Death: Stories to Move Beyond Suffering

GOD is Love

—Jesus of Nazareth

Become Your 'Values Mind'

Enlightenment is a word with many meanings. A fundamental substrata of the idea, that gives it a real foundation in human life, is the possibility that we can live our lives so that we fully engage with the part of ourselves that *is* going to **last**.

What part of us lasts? Our **values** last, in that true values grow and develop through our lives and are reflected in the lives of those around us. We can show this in *stories of value*, bringing the value alive through the experiences of the heroes in the story.

Listening to a metaphor, as we *view* the heroes of the story tackling adversity, we are able to see all elements from a wider viewpoint—a coach's viewpoint. This enables us to develop, over time, an *overview awareness*, which enables the growth of our own personal long-term values.

The 'coach position' perspective allows us to joyfully identify with others as much as with our *singular self*, and this provides both gratification and deep meaning. Yet this is not *private and personal self-identification*. It is true overview awareness when we actually link into the flow of deep appreciation for all we survey.

People don't easily imagine anything that can be *of them* that is not specifically *'of their own private self-story.'* Yet, with practice, they can learn this skill. It is a key life ability bringing a joyful 'mosaic' of experience to all aspects of our inner growth. We relax into value awareness.

This ability can transform our lives. With value awareness, we can rebuild our focus entirely which, in turn, creates inner peace. We can develop self-awareness that includes *coach position* as a deep form of participation. With many choices and a connection to inner value, we move to a place where we can relax about all possible futures as we take part in life in the moment.

In other words, we can learn to extend our life consciousness beyond individual consciousness and find both expansive awareness and inner certitude. We discover the huge joy of contribution and experience the value that gratitude provides.

We can open the *jewel box of refined awareness* each moment. Immediately, we can enjoy the depth—and the width—of our life, regardless of our current surroundings. The shackles of individual difficulties fall away, personal worries over status concerns fade, physical disabilities no longer matter, and even death becomes acceptable.

Our *Values Mind*, which is our deep intuitive field of awareness, is ever present in all of us. It is reflected in our eternal values—alive and integrous, *omnipresent* and *omniscient*. Specifically, love is love, no matter where or when it shows up. Deep awareness shines through all the moments, and life becomes peaceful.

Is not *value* infinite? How can we feel alone if our inner richness continues forever, as a field of universal value, ever expanding? How can we think ourselves as separate when our individual life is a part of this? If our value life continues like a wave on the sea, the heart of awareness also remains abundant and full. *Alone* actually means "all one."

The personal self cannot have divine experience because it considers itself as being '*only finite*.' Yet, if we take on our deep value connection and genuinely experience this through a timeless story, we learn to build the deep connection to the development of *all value* for all humanity—timeless into the future. Our stories assist to build this natural connection.

Ask yourself: What would happen if you associated with your deepest and purest values as your very *self*? Is it not possible that all dissociation would fade—that your life would become vitalized and freed?

Ask yourself: What if you associated with the joy of others and felt grateful for the opportunity? What if you 'stepped in' to enjoy their joy? Is it not possible that your life would become rich, warm, and sunny, like a beautiful day?

Solution-Focused Alchemy:
The Tonglin Monk

 Our vision and contexts create our world. We live in the contexts that we create.

Perhaps you have heard stories about the Alchemists of the Middle Ages transmuting base metals into gold. Similar to these tales is the story of a Buddhist monk who was famous because he began a practice of breathing in the faults, mistakes, issues and problems of everyone in the world in the form of visualized black smoke. He would then visualize breathing this out, and transmute it into a healing golden light. He taught this practice, which he called **Tonglin**, to his students.

This famous **Tonglin** monk practiced this transmutation all his life. Near the end of his life, he called his students to him and told them, with tears in his eyes, that he had a dream that he would be reborn in the realms of Buddhist heaven. He was very disappointed that he would not be born in a realm of hell where he could **really** assist people. He asked his students to pray that he would be reborn in hell where he could better do his work.

Great 'Metaphor Makers' Create Alchemy

This story of the Tonglin Monk has become an anecdote about how surprising people's models of the world can be. It is particularly useful to notice that happiness is something we create for ourselves, completely outside of any preferred context. It compels us to notice that we can relax in life and really develop happiness, moment by moment, no matter where we are or what occurs.

Alchemy refers to a process of turning base metals (such as iron) into *fine* metals (such as gold and silver). Using solution-focused coaching practices as the framework for our own form of alchemy, we are able to transform—and thereby move beyond— all types of contextual disappointment. Solution-focused alchemy means that every *realm* we enter becomes *fine* simply because we actively transmute any current *realm* into a *fine state of being*! This world in all its forms—heaven or hell—becomes a *fine* place in which to *be*!

Every realm in life can be experienced as either a heaven or a hell. Observe the people around you. Some people live joyfully so that they float lightly through life—even physical pain touches them lightly. Some are clearly living in a self-imposed purgatory—trudging through the *quicksands of life*, wearing lead boots.

In actual fact, there are no realms of content or adversity *out there*! Each realm is *within the individual*. We all have the power to be energy transformers anywhere or anytime by using solution-focused alchemy to turn our lives into gold.

Like the practice of **Tonglin** by the Buddhist monks, we coaches are all *light breathers* in that we instinctively choose to actively heal those with whom we connect, through solution-focused words and by being effectively responsive. We are practicing enlightenment one conversation at a time. In this way, words and experiences have no power to harm us. We cannot find ourselves in any form of hell. We are alchemists.

Every realm we enter becomes like gold because we actively transmute it. Solution-focused practice, as metaphor developers and as coaches, means we can commit to be active producers of light. A light producer is not a light weight optimist, but an active realist producing results through action. Light producers are active participants who participate fully in the results of people around them.

If we develop a story showing someone who creates his or her own *context of choice*, we show someone who is free. We show someone who can easily forgive others and free themselves from all kinds of disappointments. They cannot be harmed by life, whatever the scenarios they live within.

The life of such a person deeply impresses us with profound possibilities for ourselves. We, the storytellers, become as touched by the story as those who hear it. Become a light producer! **Turn lives into true gold!**

Develop Transformational Vision—Tell Stories

People have often tried to *create isomorphic metaphors*: equating one event in the story with a similar event in the life of the listener. This has proven to be a difficult task for storytellers and is not a particularly successful strategy since our lives are filled with so many unique events and unique people.

As a young woman, I was pressed by an Ericksonian specialist to create *isomorphic* metaphors. I found the skill set of isomorphism unnecessarily difficult. I didn't have a naturally dazzling storytelling capacity. In fact, I knew very little about multilevel narratives and was overwhelmed by the unnecessary detail of trying to match story and life events. After going to a workshop to learn effective, isomorphic metaphor development, I did not tell any stories at all for the two years which followed. It took a while to regain my courage.

Much more useful, I found, was a simple values approach that develops *relational* and *meaningful* level transformation through the story. I discovered that any story about value and vision could become strong and *sticky*. It could easily connect me, and others, to a transformational level of deep **purpose** and **commitment**. I found that stories with these focal points were like rocket fuel. They could create liftoff into the stratosphere of life engagement.

Transformation does not result from the tale itself or from the story outcome. The function of the story, and its events, is to stimulate *an overview position* that allows us to examine our big questions about life. This vision then transfers emotionally into an experience of *correspondence* to the quality of value and purpose in *every* life story. We all are pilgrims on the path of inner growth.

If a story details the clarification of values and vision that are truly relevant to the listener, then a transformation begins to happen naturally for that listener. This vision-value connection assists people to make powerful *identity level* shifts. Our capacity to imagine ourselves becoming stronger in our purpose and commitment is what triggers our growth.

The River Crossing

 I have taken many long walks on various trails along the Pacific Coast in my lifetime, but the one that had the most impact on my life was the very first.

As a young woman in need of some solitary time, I left my children with my family and arranged a seven-day hiking trip along a very difficult trail on the west coast of Vancouver Island. I prepared well, with a very light pack, maps, compass, and a brand new tide table, as advised. Learning the trail for three days, I discovered that it was tough slogging, with many steep climbs, ladders, and a lot of mud. Although the trail followed the Pacific Coast, it only really approached it at river mouths and campsites.

Sore and tired by the third day, I sat eating my breakfast and contemplated the beach. The tide was far, far out with flocks of gulls flying around the rocks, hunting for food.

Looking at my map, I noticed that the next campsite was only 10 miles away. Feeling my sore muscles, I hoped for a short day. I noticed that the flat, straight route beside the sea made the campsite seem much closer. "Gosh," I thought, "I should be able to walk there, along the shore, within four hours, maximum." Hopeful, I checked the tide table and noted that the tide would not be in for six hours. "Done," I said to myself. "I'm heading out, and I will go along the shore."

Have you even seen a picture of the cliffs of Dover: high and concave, with a flat stone base where the sea meets the wall? This is very similar to the cliff I now found myself walking beside.

For two and a half hours, I enjoyed the hike. I was walking primarily on flat rock and was able to explore many deep, water-filled pits containing small beautiful aquariums with colorful sea anemones and other amazing creatures. I paused often, to enjoy them. There were also large crevices or fissures in the rock floor, where it was necessary to climb down three steps and up again on the other side. I noticed there was not even one place to climb uphill to leave the beach. The cliff face blocked all connections to the upper trails.

About three and a half hours into the hike, I suddenly realized that quite a bit of water was now filling the crevices. Shocked, I checked the tide table. All this water didn't make sense. Reading the tide table more carefully, I realized that I had made a mistake. The numbers I had read that morning, from the tide table, were actually for **high** tide. In about three hours, the spot where I was standing would be covered with at least eight feet of water. I was in trouble and it was too late to go back. I had to move full speed ahead, and very fast.

As I started to run down the beach, I entered the longest hour of my life. Each time I jumped a crevice, it was filled with rushing water. Some were very wide, almost impassable. I realized, after one scary jump, that I could not go back, and might meet an impassable gorge ahead. It was slippery and very dangerous. I moved as fast as I could but the water was coming in quickly. There was nowhere to climb above it.

I began to see pictures of my funeral; my children now orphans. I began to pray, and prayed fervently: "If I survive this, my life will be of service," I promised the world. "Is it possible, please, to have this life?"

It was a long, long hour. The water rose quickly and was now flowing across the flat rock plates and approached closer to the cliff wall with each wave.

Far up ahead, I could see that the cliff curved outwards, towards the sea. "Maybe that's the river mouth," I thought. "If I move with all my might, I'm sure I can get there before the water gets me." And I did. It was a huge effort.

I was sloshing as I arrived, but I climbed the small rocks at the end of the short peninsula in about a half an hour. The band of curved stone was very low, about five feet high. Eagerly, I peered across to the other side of the peninsula.

It was indeed the river but not what I expected. I had been told to expect a river with a crossing. What I saw was a large river mouth, flooded with the incoming tide. No crossing was possible in the fierce riptide. To my dismay, I also saw that the 'Dover' cliff face continued up the river mouth for at least 200 yards, ending in a high gorge. Any possibility of moving up, beyond, or across, seemed completely blocked by the wide, swirling river itself.

Far across, on the other side, half a mile away, I saw some tents.

Painstakingly, I edged 60 feet up the river mouth until I could go no further. It was impossible to climb, for 10 feet above me were some gnarled tree branches extending from a tree higher up the cliff. I was now blocked in all directions, and the water was rising.

Suddenly I saw a man emerge, carrying dishes, from a far-off tent. He began to walk toward his side of the river. It seemed as though he suddenly became aware of me. He put the dishes down and went back to the tent. I didn't know if he wanted to help me, was ignoring me, or if he even noticed my plight. I continued to wait, hoping against all odds, that he wanted to help me. A very long 10 minutes passed.

Suddenly, he emerged from the tent with another man, and they were both carrying ropes. Then I saw them hurrying towards me, and I knew I had aid.

The next part of this story is one of the most spectacular events I have witnessed in my lifetime. Hardly looking at me, the man with the rope eyed the tree branches 10 feet above my head—a long way from him and across the river. Carefully making a lasso, like in the old cowboy movies, he twirled it above his head and threw it with all his might.

It was a perfect throw, over a vast space, and caught the broken tree branch perfectly.

There was now a rope across the swirling river.

Next, with the other rope, he made a second lasso and after several efforts to get it to me, I was able to catch it. Shouting, he told me how to tie it around my waist. Now there were two ropes: one guide rope to hold, and one holding me. With the two ropes secured, I dared to step into the surging river. I was pulled off my feet immediately, but held on and regained some footing. I moved slowly, step by step, over the rolling rocks below, with cold water swirling up to and around my neck. With help from the ropes, I was able to cross.

The two guys took no time to introduce themselves. They saw I was safe; then they scolded me. One ran back to the tent and brought me a paper blanket. That was it. I fell asleep in minutes. They were gone before I awoke that evening. I looked for them, but the tent had vanished.

> *Since that time, crossing my own inner river has been the heart of my vocation.* **We all have a river to cross in our life**: *a situation where circumstances demand our courage and our vision. And if we cross it, our life opens forward into the promises we make.*
>
> **We all have a river to cross in our life.** *Difficulties can easily sweep us off our feet. Yet if we hold firm, we can find our passageway into our next level of living!*
>
> *The rope we hold on to, to guide us, is our values. We must know them, tie them on, and really throw them to the far shore. With our values linking us to our visions and to each other, we dare to step out. We can step into the chasm of real leadership and real trust, and cross into the future of our dreams.* **We all have a river to cross** *and, if we truly cross over, our lives open up with value and purpose to everyone around us!*

Designing a Transformational Reality

The **contract** with all metaphors is to create examples of a *life journey* that lead to expanded potentials not only for the hero in the story, but also—at a deeper level—for all of us who listen to the story. Through hearing the story, we begin to develop the internal connections needed to build a reality. We link together what is real and valid for the journey we personally are exploring right now and, at the same time, for all of life in general. We discover our own inner truth.

By telling the story, we are *reminding* people, moving them towards their own authentic journey. We are assisting them to open their *mind of inner awareness* to an overview of their own journey, a journey of transformational self-exploration and development.

The Story of Uriah Millard

 Let me tell you the story of Uriah Millard. He shares the same name as my birth name, Millard, and for about eight years he was a proud, if not unusual, member of my New Brunswick forefathers' family. His story has deeply touched mine. There is a powerful link across time to the wonderful courage and vision his story has inspired in my life.

Uriah was a black boy from Rio de Janeiro. I first saw his strong, young face in my grandfather's family album. I heard my grandfather's voice catch with emotion when I asked whom the boy with the big smile and bright black eyes could be. "That's Uriah," he murmured softly.

Picture the scene. I was sitting on my grandfather's porch on a bright spring morning. Looking up, I saw his eyes filled with tears. "Who is he?" I asked, looking at another photo of eight boys in hockey uniforms, with black Uriah standing proudly in front with his wide smile and flashing eyes. My old grandfather, with a far-off look in his eye, began to tell an amazing story:

"My father built clipper ships," he said. "In fact, he built the biggest and best clipper ships in the world. He built them right there in New Brunswick! And we used these great boats to take Canadian fish and other products down to South America, where we traded them and returned with all sorts of South American goods.

"When I was eleven, I went on the trip of my life on one of these boats. I was the youngest of eleven children and my father thought I was old enough to be the Captain's helper. Four weeks later, after the ship landed in Rio, the Captain told me it would take a month to reload the vessel and that I was free to play until we again set sail. The first friend I met was Uriah. He was a pier scavenger who ran errands for the sailors and boat people. He also spoke English."

My grandfather's voice became animated as he described the adventure. His eyes lit up as he talked about touring the wharves and streets of Rio with Uriah. He waved his hands and described the colors, sounds, and smells of the port section where they played.

"Uriah was my age," he said, "but he was a free agent. His mother had returned to her village in the mountains because she was ill. Uriah wanted to go to school somewhere, learn to read, become a doctor, and find a way to heal her. That's why he had practiced hard and learned English from the sailors on the wharf.

"He was a really clever boy," mused my grandfather. "He could always find work for food. And he was lots of fun. We played lots of games. He loved to swim. He was a great swimmer and was teaching me. And I was teaching him to read."

At this point, watching my grandfather, I realized he was far-off inside himself, visualizing his life as a boy. He was being that boy again.

He continued: "The boat needed repairs, and so it was two months later when the Captain finally announced we would sail the next morning. Uriah stepped forward and asked if he could join the crew as a ship's helper. The Captain laughed. "We don't bring street kids from Rio de Janeiro to Canada," he said.

We sailed that afternoon. Uriah stood and waved at me awhile, as they worked loose the anchor. Then he disappeared.

The next morning, the steward found Uriah under a barrel on the deck. Grandfather's eyes twinkled as he recalled the scene!

"Everyone was upset but me. We were still in the river mouth, so they decided to put him ashore while it was yet possible. The small boat set off, landed, disembarked Uriah, and returned. Our ship continued on its way, this time heading far out to sea. Then, the next day, once again, they found Uriah under another barrel!"

This time there was no talk of returning him. No one even asked how he got back on the ship. Uriah peeled potatoes and onions in the galley for four weeks, and we continued home to Canada.

"When we landed my family took him in—no question." Then his voice became firm and proud. Uriah explained his story about how he wanted to learn to read and become a doctor and my father said: "Why not! Stay with us, go to school, and see if you can make it."

Grandfather continued: "Uriah covered four years of school in six months. In two years, he was in junior high school with the rest of us. He was a super athlete. He very quickly became the captain of our school hockey team. He was very fast and very strong and won a lot of games," he said, pointing to the picture of the boy with flashing black eyes. "He was a lot of fun and the whole family was proud of him. We loved him a lot.

"He got top marks in the high school exams and when he finished high school, he was accepted into pre-medical school." At this point, grandfather's tone changed. He continued on with the story, in a soft voice.

"The summer that Uriah was accepted into pre-med, my father built the last great Clipper ship. It was a beauty, very, very big, with rows and rows of sails. Laden with goods, it stood proudly in the harbor awaiting its christening and departure to South America. Uriah decided to take this opportunity to return to Rio one last time, to look for his mother."

Then I noticed grandfather was crying. Grandfather paused in his story and wiped his tears away. "It was a great launch. The band played a Maritime hymn and the ship sailed grandly out of the harbor, with people waving from the cliffs and steeples.

"The boat never arrived. It was found one month later, overturned somewhere in the Bermuda Triangle, capsized with water washing over it, but not fully sunk! Only one person had survived, initially, by living on flying fish for 10 full days. They found his body tied to the boat hull with a rope. It was Uriah. Each day, he had carved a short message on the boat hull, counting off the days, hoping for rescue." My grandfather paused, his voice was sad yet sounded proud: "On the tenth day, he carved his last message. He wrote his own epitaph, a short statement: 'Uriah Millard, 1892 to 1910: **Life was a Great Adventure!**'"

At first, Uriah's story was my grandfather's story. From time to time, I replayed it in my mind, seeing again the proud face and the warm eyes of the black boy with the hockey team. Gradually, however, I took the story to my heart and I asked myself: "What if I could live

> *a life with such courage, too? What if I could say proudly: 'Life was a great adventure?'"* So I whispered to Uriah in my heart: *"I will carry you forward into mine. I will honor your promise. I will practice your courage. I will discover the true future we share. Oh, Uriah, I will make for you a great adventure. For myself, and for us all:* **Let life be a great adventure!***"*

Kayaking Images and the Heartbeat of Life

Let us use an example from a story I often tell while conducting a workshop for couples. Imagine that you are about to tell a story to a room full of people. You talk about the various processes of breathing comfortably and at the same time, you begin to describe the details of a journey involving a day of rhythmic kayaking.

You speak *rhythmically*, describing the *slow, even splash of the oars*. If we had physiology monitors on the group, before too long these monitors would show that most of the people have quickly entered a state of relaxed rhythmic breathing as they listen inwardly to their rhythmic *inner oars*. They will *hear* the *splash of the oars* as part of their own *inner rhythm*. They will envision the image of a serene kayaking trip. They will breathe deeper and more rhythmically, in tune with the peacefully splashing oars that they see and hear in their mind's eye.

Suppose you build an image of a couple happily boating together. You might begin to talk in many different ways about breathing comfortably in unison. Meanwhile, you expand the vision of rhythmic kayaking partnership. In this way, you can link and associate all couple relationships to that easy pace and to *mind's eye images* of peaceful rhythmic awareness.

Perhaps your images could also invoke other areas of peaceful relationships. You shift the field of awareness and possibly access the partners who are engaging with the story. Through your story, you assist people to float to the values level of their inner awareness, to re-associate, and to rebuild relaxation and rhythm to their own definition and experience of partnership. These ideas are incompatible with the old memories of two people who have jagged emotions and fragmented, negative thoughts about each other, so the old ideas become replaced with serene, relaxed images. You can also assist people in linking and associating to peaceful physical responses and strong relaxation levels. The images and the rhythm make it impossible for them to move back to stress or habituate the stressful state of being—very much like the practice of meditation.

Through such a multilevel story, you can bring back powerful yet familiar states of positive relationship linked both to the physical body and to the idea of partnership itself. Both you and your listeners experience release and re-association into rhythmic relational awareness.

In summary, a story can be used to put key images together that unfold and link together important values, attitudes, and mindsets. These lead to physical and emotional changes that support transformational growth. This gradually develops into a heightened capacity for many kinds of refined awareness not just relaxed rhythm with a partner. With practice, we develop the nervous system linkages needed to maintain these capacities.

The Bengal Tiger Under the Bed

Because Milton Erickson lived with 40 years of muscle spasms from childhood polio, he knew pain, and he knew a lot about using visualization to work with physical discomfort. A woman in the last stages of a very painful cancer once asked him to help her. She did not want to take pain medication because she felt it would not allow her to access her creative mind. She asked Milton for an alternative.

Milton responded, "Madam, this may be easier than you think. It's something you can do for yourself, and it only takes a moment's practice. Pretend for a moment that you notice a slight movement at your door, which is ajar. As you look up, a large Bengal tiger comes into the room, eyeing you, and tensing his muscles in preparation to strike. Now tell me, as you consider this tiger, do you feel any pain?"

> "Why no," said the woman in surprise. For the next month, until she died, she used this visualization, and other similar ones, as an effective method of pain control. Whenever people asked her about her pain, she would simply reply, "I'm managing okay. I simply keep a large Bengal tiger under the bed."

Washing Away Entitlement: A Meditation

Step into the sacred river of truth for a moment and feel the swirling current of true life all around you. Notice the special blessing quality of these waters as you sense and give your life to the river's potency. Notice that, as it begins to wash over you, you gradually melt off the crusts of *entitlement* that you have formed over yourself as protection.

Watch the entitlement habits slowly wash downstream and leave you. Allow all your entitlements to float off and wash down the river—your entitlement to wealth, to comfort, to protection, to safety, to beauty, to the ownership of things, and even to the ownership of your body.

Watch your petulant hopes float away and disappear. Watch the river carry them all off—the crusts of expectation, the filters of blindness, the rags of clinging—all swept off and away in the powerful stream of awareness that moves you beyond old boundaries and requirements.

Maybe you have considered yourself entitled to clear roadways, good service, or respect. Maybe you have come to expect great health or adulation from others. Where do your hidden expectations grab evaluative thoughts and create negative emotions? Wash them all away.

Find yourself standing naked in the truth of awareness. Be totally grateful for this opportunity to be alive just as you are and for the opportunity to be true to this tender new, genuine aliveness. See, hear, and feel the moment, as it is—a singular precious gift. This moment is different from any before it. This **now** needs our tender awakened awareness to come alive.

Naked, we are born. Naked, we hold hands together on the journey and, only naked, we can step into this sacred river of true life.

Chapter 6

Connecting to Inner Truth

*The means and the ends are always of the same.
Become the change you want to see in the world!*

—Mahatma Gandhi

Building a New Mind

We need to build a new mind systemically in order to inhabit and use it well, in the same way that we need to build a house systemically in order to inhabit it and use it well.

Consciousness metaphors allow us to quickly build advanced awareness. We can always *build* a new mind—the mind is wonderfully metaphoric! We can build a mind for a day, for a year, for our lifetime, or for a universe of lifetimes. All one has to do is ponder on the mind they wish to build and focus on the decisions they want that mind to make. The mere act of focusing will attract whatever is the focus.

What mind do you wish to inhabit today?

Stories are like containers—you and others will immerse fully in the story that you are telling. You will also live in the mind that you build for others. You must decide how you will the build the mind you will live in through your story. Think of your own *widest awareness* as you begin to build.

- Visualize the mind you are building as a wave in the sea.
- You are in your own wave, but also can see beyond it to the wider ocean.
- Notice that you are experiencing oneness with the entire ocean of consciousness.
- Enjoy the wave and the wide ocean of awareness all at the same time.
- Notice that you and they are one and the same.

What *size of mind* do you want your metaphor to assist people to live within?

What values do you want them to experience and enjoy?

What are the possibilities on which you can focus?

What areas particularly interest you?

- Is it a mind of compassion?
- Is it a mind of happiness?
- Is it a mind of balanced integrity?
- Is it a mind of peaceful observation and awareness?

- Is it a mind of joyful play?
- Is it a mind of true value?

Here is a recipe to try for fun:

Build access to inner truth and value through your story; then widen the size of your mind far beyond. Stretch even to the size of the Universe—beyond the size of a thousand galaxies. Relax and share the meaning and potency of this great awareness, vast and value-laden, that you inhabit—through your story! When you stretch, your voice stretches and everyone can feel it.

The Significant Power of Promising

A key area in which transformational conversations have great power is in clarifying an inner promise. People sometimes hide from their inner development by using holding patterns, fears, and inward lies based on *old conclusions*. The universe comes along and pokes a hole in the façade—often during sickness or crisis. The word *universe* means "one song." When we lose our inner *music*, the *one song* can come to **re-mind** us!

By telling a transformational story, we bring people back to their inner music. We become a catalyst for renewal, assisting others to glimpse and then to explore their strongest values and vision. Once again, we become a lighthouse guiding the way to life development.

You can affect reality at the quantum level when you ***promise***. Until you promise, the unknown could turn out any number of different ways. **With a promise, you significantly lean into the magic of reality making.**

Quantum means "… an indivisible entity of energy." In the realm of all possible alternatives, the universe has a random quality. However, when we truly promise a significant result, we shift the statistics powerfully. We become **re-minded**!

The *observer* makes all the difference with quantum choices. A *coach position* is important with these choices. We need to *overview* them. It all seems like it is only a discovery, yet **what we look for tends to be what we actually find**. This can be seen in cancer survivors, whose tumors suddenly shrink and disappear when the person becomes empowered with a compelling purpose.

What is interesting is that people in remission can always describe a *significant moment of true promising* at some point before the remission took place. **Re-mission** is exactly that! We promise to engage with a mission of value and we go *into* remission. Then we need to **re-member** to build this into our physical experience.

The Grand Canyon Wall

One woman, in a seminar I was teaching, reported to me that her doctors had just discovered a large tumor in her liver and told her the tests showed it was inoperable. She did a 'vision walk' with my assistance. In her inner process, she described a high wall between herself and her life, her future, and even her values. She stopped in the middle of the process and physically sagged. She sighed.

"What if you climb over the wall?" I asked. "Or go around it?"

"It stretches forever like the Great Wall of China," she said, "and it's as high as the Grand Canyon."

"Are you climbing it now?" I asked, engaging her in the active part of the process.

She nodded. "It's very high; too high."

"What possibility, what choice will make climbing over this wall easier?" I asked.

"That I use my life for something useful," she muttered. She paused for a minute, and then softly said, "But I don't know what."

"What might you promise to yourself?" I asked. "Is it worth it? What if this time you really find the true purpose for your life?"

She nodded, and bit her lip; then suddenly started to physically relax. "I did promise," she said, "Even if I don't know!" The furrow departed from her brow, and she straightened and stretched. "I'm reaching the top of the wall," she said. "It is easier." A moment later

> she added: "On the other side is a lot of light. Now I'm over. I've really got a vision." For five minutes she stood radiant in her inner awareness.
>
> Later she discussed the experience as a breakthrough. She explained to all others that she didn't know what it meant yet, but she needed it and got it. Now she was waiting to discover what was next.
>
> In fact, when she went for x-rays and tests next, her tumor wasn't there! Her future was, however, and she enrolled in college classes towards a new career.

Promising Brings Results

One way for a person to move forward is to *speak their promise to life with presence and authority*. We, as coaches, affirm people when we ask them to search for and find what is truly authentic and real for them. We need to encourage and challenge them to head directly towards that reality.

People need to ask themselves:
- What truth needs to be revealed that clarifies my purpose and authentic evolutionary aims?
- What is the true meaning of my life, and how can I get on track to my purpose?

For some people, discovering the ***power of promising*** provides a huge turning point in their life. Promising significantly raises our capacity for changing our reality. Discovering this power allows you to begin to make choices as if they really matter in the universe.

In our stories, we can ask the question: *"What might you promise to yourself?"*

This is a great question and impacts our metaphor powerfully when we describe how the person reveals their inner aim and then speaks their promise to themselves. Life flows towards an authentic promise given to an empowered vision.

Helen Keller:
How to Create a 'Human' Mind

Many people have read Helen Keller's life story and are amazed at the intelligence, curiosity, and humor of this joyous woman who could neither see nor hear. I first read her wonderful biography on a spring day while sitting in a lawn chair, under a cherry tree laden with bright pink blossoms, and listening to the birds. I briefly tried to imagine what life would be like without functioning ears and eyes. It was hard to imagine.

Helen described her early childhood without words as living in the gray zone of 'no life' and 'no world.' She said, "I didn't know what it meant to be human. I was a small animal who slept with the dogs and reached for food from my mother's plate."

When she was seven years old, a sign language teacher came to her parents' farm to patiently work with her over the summer. Helen described a great moment of breakthrough when she first understood the idea of language. Out by the yard water tap where she drank with the dogs, the patient teacher tapped the word 'water' into her hand. She felt the sign for the word 'water' in her palm for the fortieth time, and suddenly realized what a word was! She raced back to the house, pulling the teacher by the hand. She now wanted the signals for everything. She wanted to bring the world alive with words.

Helen loved words from that moment on! She cherished them, and the inner vision that they brought her. This quickly replaced her former 'human blindness.' She became a famous teacher and an indefatigable promoter of humanity's capacity for developing happiness. She became famous for her stunning, wise, and wonderful writing.

Helen hated to be pitied. At one point, she admonished someone: "Having no eyes or ears is livable. Far better than a life without vision." To another: "Life is a banquet. Most of us are beggars."

> *Some quotes from Helen adorn my life:*
>
> *"Your success and happiness lies in you. Resolve to keep happy and, with your joy, you form an invincible host against difficulties."*
>
> *And: "Life is either a daring adventure, or is nothing!"*

King Midas and True Value

We all know the story of King Midas. A version of the story tells how a satyr gave the king two wishes in return for a favor he had provided. Midas responded with glee. "I want a road across the land," said the King. The satyr bowed and a beautiful stone road immediately appeared, linking cities and towns just the way the King had always wanted.

The King was filled with great satisfaction, elation, and a sense of power, but also a sense of fear for the next wish was his last. "Hmm, only one more wish," he thought. "There are many other items to produce—palaces and bridges. What can I do to preserve this opportunity?"

Inspired, he spoke his wish. "From this time forth, let everything I touch turn to gold," he requested. The satyr bowed. The goblet the king was holding had already turned to gold.

The king was very happy with his new power. He wandered through the palace, touching throne and tables, curtains and vessels, seeing them turn to gold before his eyes. Suddenly his small daughter, the light of his life, appeared, joyfully running towards him with her arms open. As was his habit, he lovingly opened his arms to grasp her to his breast. To his horror, she immediately turned to gold. "What have I done?!" cried the king. "My wonderful child is now forever gone!"

> He asked the gods to be relieved of his gift. Dionysus heard him and relented. If he bathed in the River Pactolus, and gave all that he had to those who had nothing, perhaps his good deeds would be rewarded by the Gods with a third wish.
>
> Midas did so. He rushed to give the command to sell all of his gold to purchase food and medicines for the common people. He emptied his private storerooms, buying more necessary items for the people throughout the land. He did not hesitate to sell his palaces and all of his possessions, until all that he had once owned was almost gone.
>
> At this time, the satyr appeared once more. "You have been given a third wish by the Gods and even a fourth for your efforts." Much relieved, the King used a wish to release his beloved daughter. "I thank you with all my heart," he said to the satyr. "As for my fourth wish, I have already received it. I am grateful to have learned what **true value is**. That it is more precious than anything gold can purchase."
>
> What is more precious than any gold you could accumulate? What is truly valuable to **you**?

The Shift to Personal Development

Our conscious mind has evolved with a pattern of getting needs filled being the primary daily aim. Our ancient ancestors' primary need was for daily survival. They developed a 'periscope' in their focal mind—constantly scanning their environment for food, shelter, and tools for survival.

Later, when immediate survival was established, what did their minds focus on? They needed security—to stockpile provisions so they could rest easier. Since that time, mankind never developed the stockpile stop button. This has developed into what seems like a need for 'lots of stuff.'

Pay attention to your internal dialogue. What does the conscious mind think it wants? It thinks it wants more of what it already has and enjoys and thinks it needs.

- more personal pleasure
- more provisions and *'stuff'*

- more compassion, more love, more attention
- more entertainment

The irony is that only your deep intuitive knowing system, your beyond conscious mind, is capable of experiencing real pleasure, real learning, and real development. This it does through relaxing and relinquishing, through listening and loving.

If we are strongly identified with the conscious mind, we may not be aware of the true experience of inner awareness beyond personal identity.

Buddha once said, *"All suffering is sourced in denial."* What is Denial? *Denial is a defense mechanism. De Nile* is not a river in Egypt.

It may seem like these different levels of consciousness are working at cross-purposes. Inner conflict finally diminishes with the gradual recognition of our over-arching inner purpose. And with this comes the joyful recognition of our ongoing participation in our deeper life. This is the bond of our joint development, a place of transformation and visionary participation. When you show this awareness, when it comes alive in your story, you create a true imprint on all who hear it.

Mohandas Gandhi and Finding Forgiveness

With the murderous uprising and violence between the Hindu and Muslim population after the British left India in 1942, Gandhi was the single person trusted by all the Hindu people trying to forge plans for peace. He was the center of all the political and spiritual overtures between Hindus and Muslims, and all attempts to restore stability.

It was during this period of violence and difficulty that a Hindu man in great upset came to see Gandhi, saying that he had committed unforgivable crimes against the Muslims and was beyond the mercy of God. "The Muslims killed my wife," he said. "I was in a rage and joined the mob." He described how, as part of this armed mob, they stopped

> *a Muslim family travelling on the road and all had been killed including a small baby boy who he himself had murdered. Now, he said, there was no way he could continue to live with such blood on his hands. "I am beyond all redemption."*
>
> *"There is a way to be forgiven," said Gandhi, "but you must do exactly as I say."*
>
> *"I will do anything," said the man.*
>
> *"Then do this," said Gandhi. "Go and find a Muslim baby, an orphan whose parents have been murdered. Raise him to adulthood yourself, giving him all care and nurturing as if he was your own son. Most important," said Gandhi, "make sure you raise him as a Muslim, having him trained in all aspects of the faith. If you do this with complete love, forgiveness will be yours. The door of salvation will open to you again."*
>
> *The man, with tears in his eyes, promised to do exactly what Gandhi asked. He went back to his community and peacefully gave his life to loving and raising a child.*

Be With Each Other

People do not enjoy the fact that things end—including their own physical lives! It is often a challenge to realize that our bodies are someday going to die. Therefore, dissociation is a frequent habit for people when they think towards their eventual physical dissolution.

When people dissociate from the awareness of death, it means they lose the ability to truly listen deeply to another person. The simple suffering of others pulls up this awareness. It is only when we rebuild this capacity that we can genuinely listen to others. When we realize the importance of all aspects of our human lives, we can become strong coaches.

When we are able to authentically '*be with another*,' we have reached true awareness. On the deepest level, this means **to be with** what **we** truly are. We are all companions on this journey to awareness. We are all pilgrims on the path.

For all of us, this means, metaphorically, to *stay associated to others*. It means that we become aware of what *others* feel as they face difficulty or even death. We no longer express *objections* to that awareness. We stay *with them* and do not dissociate into our own private realm. This means that we learn to do the same for ourselves. In this way, we commit to the full expression of our lives.

> ### St. Francis and the Leper
>
> There is a story from Middle Ages of St. Francis walking on a road during a long journey. In a desolate area, he finds a leper beside the road, very ill from his disease. The man is feebly signaling his need for help.
>
> Finding both the wounds and facial disfigurations of the man horrifying, St. Francis moved past quickly, pretending not to see him. Immediately his conscience smote him. After 100 meters, he turned back resolutely. He found the man and tended to his wounds. He gave him water and slowly fed him. He blessed him. The man sat up and reached towards him with his leprous hands. This time, he held them. The man transformed into Jesus.

Suffer Self-Knowledge

It has been said that there are four kinds of self-knowledge:
1) There is *what we know, we know*.
   This is the *knock-on-wood* physical world—I know my own body.
2) There is *what we know, we don't know*.
   I know that I don't know how to fly a 747 jetliner, but I could learn.

3) There is *what we don't know, that we know.*
   I don't know my inner knowledge of how to balance when I walk—yet this knowledge runs my behavior and habits in a manner that is totally trustworthy.

4) There is *what we don't know, that we don't know.*
   I don't yet know all the aspects of consciousness in my potential to unfold.
   I don't know all the ways I can expand my capacity to give, support, encourage, and assist others.

Through a strong story, we integrate and unfold the four types of knowledge. In a great story, we are truly *with* all four aspects of *being*—experiencing intuitively from inner self-knowledge. This means we integrate inner knowledge and we 'suffer' awareness of all aspects of inner knowledge. We learn to discover and unfold our inner truth.

Chapter 7

Integrity and Commitment

*I may be a despicable little man,
but when the truth speaks through me,
I am invincible!*

—Mahatma Gandhi

Metaphors That Point

A consciousness metaphor can link vision and language together to talk effectively to the whole self. Such a metaphor provides an opportunity to link **perception** and **self-discovery**, and **to point with them** to what is needed for true growth. It is similar to baseball hero Babe Ruth's famous gesture of 'pointing over the center field fence.'

A story will delineate and train people to experientially recognize some key postures, tones, and images for different qualities of consciousness and awareness. These may need some 'pointing to,' especially in the beginning.

Pointing to self-discovery is like watching for signs of spring. We learn to pay attention to the weather or *mind system* in our lives that we may be currently passing through and *determine* for ourselves that *spring* has truly arrived. Yet we must *declare* it. We must *point*. When we strongly point and declare it, we give ourselves a new beginning.

Pointing Over the Fence: Declaring 100% Commitment

Imagine sitting in overview position from the skybox of the stadium and being able to look down on the greatest baseball batter of the early twentieth century! You would see Babe Ruth of the legendary New York Yankees.

Zoom in on one great occasion: Yankee Stadium full of Babe Ruth fans. Recognize Babe, a big man with a wide grin, swaggering up to the plate before the cheering throng while the pitcher paces nervously. Watch Babe systematically testing the bats and playfully waving to the crowd.

Babe, finally ready, motions to the crowd to quiet down, and the stadium moves from noise to silence. Now, observe him as he raises his hand and points high over the outfield fence with a defiant gesture.

The crowd roars. On the very first pitch, with a smooth and mighty swing of his bat, this is exactly where he sends the ball!

*Notice Babe Ruth's gesture as a metaphorical **declaration**, to himself and all assembled, that he promised a 100% result. It created a 'thinking space' for all involved, to 'intend' together, to produce that specific result. Such a commitment can develop a powerful engagement for everyone: an arena for joint creation and the step-by-step unfolding of both the inner and outer result. This 'flow of unfolding,' which engages 100% commitment, is what follows.*

Where in your life do you create 100% commitment to a result, no matter what? As children, we do that all the time. Watch a toddler determinedly learning how to walk or talk. 100% commitment is what compels. Watch great sportsmen focused on an Olympic championship! 100% commitment points us 'over the fence'!

Emotional Renewal to Positive Energy

A powerful story tends to be experienced through our sensory channels: *sight*, *touch*, and *sound*. In this sense, a strong story is like a recipe that instructs us how to renew complete full-bodied awareness—especially if the ingredients include major difficulties.

The story of Vitaly, the builder, which follows next, is a great example of such a recipe. It tends to impact and develop the wider range of our inner awareness. It links into many aspects of inner exploration. Emotional renewal begins as we watch people renew their lives—despite all the obstacles. We feel a burst of positive energy.

The Flow of Vision:
Building the Russian 'Town'

This is the story of an event that happened in Russia in 2001. There was an economic crisis in the fragile new business culture developing in Moscow, and the Russian rouble collapsed to one-tenth of its value overnight.

In December, Vitaly, a business leader who had become my friend, found that he was about to go bankrupt with his half-completed 10,000-unit apartment city just outside of the Moscow district limits. The circle of buildings had well-designed architectural appeal, and was being built to surround playgrounds and gardens. Yet suddenly there were no potential buyers.

Vitaly was caught in a gridlock. The project depended on the continuous cash purchases of apartments, to pay the workmen. Now, with the economic crisis, the buyers had disappeared and the workers had not been paid for three months. Furthermore, there was a major conflict brewing between the construction managers and sales managers of the company. Everyone debated how to regain the trust of the customers. Most urgently, the company's financial framework was failing. It had no funds to sustain the business, or even to pay for the heating of its headquarters.

Vitaly, the owner and project leader, begged me to speak to his managers. He was certain I could do some magic and keep them all onboard. With eyes uplifted, he stood before me: "You can arouse them," he said. "It is a great project and with your help we will get it done!"

His hands went up in the air, and he opened his palms in a great, emphatic, and visionary gesture! His voice, trembling yet strong, proclaimed: "We have the vision! The team can stay together! The town will rise. The gardens will be planted!"

Vitaly truly inspired me with his deep commitment. I wondered how his people would respond. He hired a car to drive me from central

Moscow to their main office, where the employees had gathered. On arrival, I found that the heating for the entire building had just been turned off that very morning because the utility bill had not been paid. I was ushered into a large, freezing-cold auditorium filled with despondent people wearing coats, scarves, and mittens.

How do we begin when people have become sad and cynical? Fortunately, my friend Vitaly, the project leader, knew how to start the conversation. He spoke briefly and urgently to the group about 'the day of making choices.' Then he turned to me to speak, calling me the 'fire lighter'!

How do we re-engage vision in the dispirited? We need to ask for it vigorously and on all logical levels; vision, identity, values, capabilities, actions, and environment. We can also develop a visual metaphor for an inner contract. It needs to be a valid and valuable description of our own strong intention. I wondered what vision could move them. I wondered how, as their spokesperson, I could also find that.

I started speaking to the group, noting that they were a courageous crew: people committed to a big result. What kind of contract had they made for their own success?

I inquired about the spirit they had formerly brought to the project. What vision, what mission had called them to this enterprise? What values had got them started? What kind of a story were they building—even beyond the architecturally amazing super-structures that were rising towards the sky?

In plain terms, I asked them to continue their project contract and to get the project done "even in these difficult times." People remained quiet in the cold auditorium, yet clearly they were listening! No one spoke.

New contracts for success can begin with metaphors of renewal, especially if they are self-declared. After giving a few examples, I requested one from the gathered group. Several people spoke of their pride in the enterprise, building a great community.

Playfully, I asked them for a visual metaphor for that original intent. What image or mascot picture would come to mind if they *were to find one? I also asked for one that fit the new circumstances! Several people suggested a few standard metaphors: a beehive, a garden, and a wheel hub. Nothing appealed to the group, but they began to show some interest in the idea. They had worked hard and the ideas stimulated their pride.*

Then someone spoke with the real truth of the moment: "We are like a group of miners digging for ore in the Siberian tundra. The ore is deep below the permafrost and we are isolated in the wilderness. It's like we are alone. We are out here in the cold tundra, digging alone."

It was immediately clear that everyone loved this analysis. It rang with reality! I playfully started drawing a tent city on a large white board, using a strong black marker. I added deep digging pits, and showed the fierce wind blowing, with strong lines. Clearly, they approved and had me add more lurid details to the images: lonely tents and piled snow.

I continued to detail my picture. Now, I began to add some new features. I emphatically put a 'cook tent' in the middle of the tents, with warm orange light shining from the windows. I showed a broad path from the 'construction crew's tent' and the 'sales crew's tent' to this warm central 'cook tent.' The more I embellished the metaphor and added connecting paths, friendly light, and windows on the tents, the more animated the group became. There was a flow of energy in the room now. People continued telling me what to add to the picture. I showed a group of donkeys pulling carts, ready to leave for the city with piles of golden ore. They particularly liked the image of piles of the golden ore waiting in the donkey carts!

We continued to play with the image for about half an hour. They knowingly discussed a few of the difficult factors of 'life in the tundra' and everyone laughed. I pointed to the warm-looking cook tent and asked if it was big enough. They laughed some more as I added more large, warm, bright windows to it. They asked me to pile more ore on the donkeys' carts and all roared as I piled them two meters high, to the top of the large white board, and colored them brightly with yellow highlighter.

> When I was leaving, I could see that the group had visibly relaxed. I learned later that critical conversations were had, negotiations were completed, and the employees had agreed to stay and work until the flow of money resumed. The 'tundra workers' were rewarded with their own apartments once the 'ore' had been delivered.

How People Grow New Capacities

Our inner experience of transformation is retrieved when you, the metaphor creator, detail transformational examples. The listener will naturally transfer these to their personal self. They *foresee* possibilities of value through the story. This creates new linkages in the brain, which they can use to develop further associative recollection and personal links to their own life.

The story allows a person to experience and connect to their inner world of experience through rich associative perceptions. Neurologically, people always experience the world by way of their bodies. Visual detailing creates internal self-image linkages to the actions of both our own values and our physical experiences.

The 'Teddy Bears Picnic'

How do we develop the risk-taking habit? We need to promise it. We need to promise courage and promise action. The viral seeding of the risk-taking promise is an interesting feature of effective coaching. If I were to tell you that developing this one habit—to visualize and promise risk-taking action—could move you towards your goals ultra **fast**, would that interest you?

"All life is an experiment. The more experiments you make, the better," said Ralph Waldo Emerson. Re-engaging the risk-taking vision is a key part of re-energizing all personal power. To be adverse to risk means more and more habituated focus on roles and rules and, in turn, creative promising dies. With this, excitement dies. As Bobby Dylan, the twentieth-century songwriter once twanged, "He who isn't busy being born is busy dying."

I once pondered this as I looked at my broken garden. A risk-taking bear, three long blocks from his mountain home, had just crashed into my garden and been shot with anesthetic by a wildlife ranger, then unceremoniously dragged out to the street on a tarp and into a van, leaving a huge swath of broken plants! Surveying the damage, I was reminded of a long string of risk-taking bear associations that included climbing in the mountains, carrying my trusty can of bear spray. To explore British Columbia's mountains means preparing to meet 'The Bear.' We have lots of bears, yet most of us still hike in these mountains.

My favorite song as a 5-year-old child was 'Teddy Bears Picnic,' a funny kid's song about going in disguise through the woods to see the bears in frivolous action—a risky vision for a preschooler. Through enrolment in a Sufi program in my early thirties, I learned to promise courage and take action 'beyond the old comfort zones.' The aim of all participants was to do one 'outrageous thing' per day beyond their comfort zones. That required thinking outside the box!

One particular Sunday while I was participating in this group, I found myself agreeing to sing a children's song to 4,000 people at a July 1st Canada Day celebration. Stepping out onto the small stage before 1,000 children in the audience, I decided to give them a romping, stomping version of 'Teddy Bears Picnic,' the only children's song I knew. I used emphatic gestures, lots of risk-taking emphasis, and a strong tone of action-excitement! My voice was carried over huge loudspeakers, across a half mile of people, and the kids loved it!

If you go down in the woods today you're sure for a big surprise
If you go down in the woods today you'd better go in disguise
For every bear that ever there was will gather there for certain
Because *today's the day the Teddy Bears have their picnic!*

It was an exhilarating discovery to learn, on that spot, that I could be a successful singer for children, when I needed to be. But even if the risk had not worked out, even if the audience had not enjoyed my brave foray into children's entertainment, I found the exercise itself to be a stimulant. It led to a wonderful, intoxicating, deep understanding that I could dare and do anything. With 'risk-taking' action now in my inner 'life agreement,' I began to dare to imagine big, plan big, assume big, and, in this way, trigger the entrepreneurial spirit in myself and in those around me. My creative vision was engaged, and the fire of provocative thinking was lit. All this, by learning to playfully promise to jump into action at the first opportunity.

I challenge you: Have you taken a risk lately?

> Whatever you can do or dream you can, begin it.
> Boldness has genius, power, and magic in it!
> — Johann Wolfgang von Goethe

Chapter 8

Your 'Integrity-Identity' As a Field of Consciousness

Everything interpenetrates everything else.
—David Bohm, quantum physicist

Expanding Identity—Who Are We?

The word **identity** comes from the Latin term *idem*, which means "the same—the sameness of essential or generic character in different examples or instances." It is our *identity* which organizes our life's **purpose**, **capabilities**, and **behaviors** into one complete system.

Identity ideas are the deepest beliefs we have that define us as individual objects located in time and space. Expanding our self-awareness always involves asking the key question, "*Who am I?*" The answers that we find determine our *integrity* and therefore our *identity*—which are one and the same!

People spend their entire lives designing an effective identity. We are always at work evaluating, exploring, and creating a more truthful self-awareness. We are always discovering more about our surprising inner consciousness and our decisions about which of our identity aspects should be pursued and developed. We gradually explore and refine the multiple '*life stories*' that we have created. When we ask ourselves, "*Who am I*," the surprises we find are astonishing.

What Is Integrity?
Abraham Lincoln's Choice!

How do we create integrity?

Integrity often requires difficult inner confrontations where we fiercely stick to our aims and values in the face of strong inner pulls to dissociate from the plan, to change it, or to quit. A good example is the interesting story of Abraham Lincoln in the last weeks of an important race for a key legislative seat.

It had been a tight race and in the final weeks before the vote, the finances for publicity and travel for Lincoln's party were almost gone. Meanwhile, the competition was still neck and neck. Lincoln's party supporters and aides were scraping the bottom of the barrel. The wealthy opposition, on the other hand, was placing full-page ads in all the newspapers and scheduling rallies in the town halls of cities throughout the country.

All at once, it seemed like the needed cash to win the race could be at hand. A wealthy man suggested he might be willing to make available the funds necessary to continue the campaign. He arrived at the party headquarters and was quickly ushered into Lincoln's office. The door was shut, and Lincoln's support personnel hovered around outside hoping for the best. Everyone dreamed that this man would provide the critical money that would Lincoln to have a fighting chance to win the race.

Suddenly, the door was flung open, and the man walked quickly away. He had his head down and his fists clenched, and he did not look back. The supporters looked around to see Lincoln slowly exit his office, with a sad face. "What happened?" they demanded. Lincoln carefully chose his words and spoke with a strained voice. "Every man has his price," he said, "and this gentleman came just a little too close to mine."

We are truly such supporters and team players, us human beings. We work hard and give to each other far beyond the call of 'required.' The next story is an example of the willingness to bring aid, far above and beyond the call of duty.

The Man in the Red Jacket

Picture Beijing airport, the largest airport in the world, after a storm in central China. There have been 79 flights cancelled. Marilyn and Lawrence have arrived from Vancouver at 4 p.m., only to discover that the next part of their trip, Beijing to Shenzhen, is in total disarray. They are told that the next available flight out will be the following afternoon, landing about six hours after Marilyn's Coaching program—with 50 students attending from all over China—is scheduled to begin.

Now, what would you do with this information? The storm had now passed but the rebookings had filled every plane, even before the flight from Vancouver had arrived to Beijing.

I, Marilyn, became determined to get on an evening flight somehow. We began to search for a means to that end but met with polite dismissal at every turn, by people with minimal English. We were sent from counter to counter, speaking to flight supervisor after flight supervisor. Again and again (six or seven times), they studied itineraries, and checked our options. Again and again we were turned away. We were told very politely that all planes were full. We filled out wait-list after wait-list—all to no avail.

Two hours passed quickly with these efforts. The first two evening flights had gone, leaving only one remaining. To make matters worse, everyone we spoke to were non-English responders. My Elite Card meant nothing in this context.

What would you do in such a situation, with all options booked? My husband Lawrence and I looked at each other and I said determinately, "We need help! There must be a way!"

At that moment, an official, in a uniform with a red jacket and lots of brass buttons, came up to us and said politely, in perfect English, "I've been observing you two. Is it possible you need some assistance?"

I poured out my story and for once, someone seemed to understand. He carefully looked at our tickets and Elite Card, then at his watch. "Let's make it happen," he said. "I know exactly how to do it." I looked into his strong brown eyes and knew that he meant it, and believed he knew what to do. I was swept with inner faith and my courage returned.

Immediately, he moved into action. "Follow me," he said, turning a key to a door leading down a stairwell that moved out of the large hall. Suddenly, we found ourselves in a labyrinth of small halls that led to tiny elevators, multiple floors, and finally to a small 'Air Canada' office—the airline we had arrived on. It was 8:30 p.m. and one woman, alone, sat in the office.

*The man in the red jacket handed her our tickets. The two immediately began to act like a football coach and quarterback in the final ten minutes of a game. She started on telephones. He set out running to the 'third basement' down below the main airport to find our luggage, tags in hand. He described this basement as a place where thousands of pieces of luggage were sent during a storm. "This is the biggest challenge," he said. "We **must** find it!" Then he confirmed the plan: "I will find your luggage and bring it here," he said strongly, "while she gets you on a flight. It will happen!" he declared with a voice full of certainty.*

Again, that feeling of deep certainty! I didn't know who he was, but he had energized this woman at the switchboard. He was taking charge. He had conviction in his voice, and I had hope.

It would be wonderful to know how they did it. I thought perhaps he was the airport general director. He behaved like he was. Within 30 minutes, he returned with our two big suitcases, while the commando woman operated the phone, making call after call in Mandarin.

Suddenly, they both hooted like a football team that had scored in the final moments. The man in the red jacket took charge once again. "We have the flight and I must get you to the gate," he said, running down the hall, pulling our two large and very heavy cases.

He got the cases, then us, to the plane in 15 minutes, racing through the airport administration areas and giving directions to a variety of people to facilitate our passage.

"Who is this guy?" I thought again: "How did we get so lucky?" He moved us straight through security, customs, and the body check, passing lines of people, and straight to the plane door... where we were expected! The plane was ready to leave.

Now came the moment of shock. He stood tall, looked Lawrence in the eye, and held out his hand. Only at this time did I realize that he was actually a porter. A porter had done this for us; a porter who moved, talked, and acted like a total leader. Lawrence, in surprise, handed over a very generous 'tip' and we boarded our plane.

Did he do this 'for the money'? Perhaps. The Universe responds in surprising ways to a 'call for help.' Did he do this for the fun? Perhaps.

> *The Universe gives amazing opportunities to build action-excitement. Did he do this out of community spirit? Perhaps. The Universe gives wonderful outreach between all the citizens of our planet... ways to share our support and love in the critical moments.*
>
> *My experience is that, no matter what the motivation, he did this **for us**. Yes, money, fun, and support were involved, but the heart has deeper reasons. The deepest reason was simple being true to us, to his agreement to assist, and thereby to himself, in a wonderful game called giving help when asked.*
>
> *We can always do it for us: play the game fiercely **for us**. We can give our hearts, our time, our energy for us, and receive life's deepest treasures: gratitude, love, and value... **for us!***

Bring Down the Wall

The development of inner awareness is the opposite of what creates addictions. Addicted people are prisoners of their habitual inner *self-talk* about *self-limitations*. Because addicts identify with the conscious mind, it means they miss the intuitive zone—the beyond-conscious or deeper knowing mind. They therefore dissociate behind a wall.

The way to emerge from dissociation is to study our most valued moments and especially pay attention to those moments of *awakened awareness*. We notice our deep life values when we are really '*being with*' ourselves. We begin to awaken when we develop real consciousness of the *contexts* that can truly be important for our developing life. The walls become irrelevant and therefore disappear.

True Human Potential:
The Great Wall of China

Recently, on my return journey to Vancouver from Kazakhstan, I flew over the Great Wall of China. From 12,500 feet, it is possible see it stretch for hundreds of miles. As you may know, the Great Wall was eventually a failure; yet, supported by rigorous efforts for 500 years, it managed to temporarily stave off the Mongol invaders.

This seems to be true with all our regimes: to 'hold off' trouble rather than meeting and exploring beyond old frameworks. The twenty-first century is a time of huge challenge and change; and, truly, we, as humanity, need to move forcefully into action to create new choices for our children. The challenges we face, as humanity, require answers that transcend the old habits and limitations of our history and background as 'a thousand tribes and cultures.' The challenges we face today require us to truly emerge into our human potential.

As coaches, let us look ahead for a moment, as if we were able to truly see a video of the human potential we are aiming for. Suppose you could see yourself in this video of our future. See the **You** who is mature, self-consistent, and wise! See the **You** who has the energy and engaged focus, to assist everyone around you, to also refocus on the inner treasure of their one life as all life.

How do you build a bridge to that future, and hold your own hand as you make those steps forward now? Do you need a coach? If so, find one today. **Your true human potential is too important to leave it 'guarding the wall.' All walls fall.**

How do you plan to move beyond 'Great Wall Thinking'? Do you want to zoom up, like on a great balloon, and survey beyond the wall? Do you want to fly up, like a rocket ship, moving towards the spacious awareness of living truth 'beyond gravity.' Don't hold back on your true potential. **All walls fall.**

> This vision 'beyond the wall' is the promise we made to our children when we first held them in our arms. We promised them 100% commitment to their future.
>
> Let us use these next years to truly fulfill our promise to the future. Let us begin strongly; and, if we pause, simply restart at the first opportunity. Our commitment needs to be to recommit—no matter what! In this way, we promise **to take real action** on our true human potential.
>
> How will **you** truly begin?

Sustainable Planet

We will use the making of yogurt as a scientific metaphor to demonstrate the sustainability of planet Earth. Imagine a bottle of pure milk in front of you, and then imagine putting two yogurt bacilli inside that bottle. Within a few moments, you will notice that they double and then very quickly double again. Within five hours, they will almost fill the whole bottle. At the same time, the milk will become yogurt. Now, this is, of course, a wonderful thing if you want yogurt. But let us consider what actually happened and the tipping point which occurred when one thing became another. Suppose it was just sugar water and bacilli, in the same scenario. One timed hour, and all the sugar will have been consumed and the bacilli will have died.

Consider the point at which the sugar became almost completely consumed by the bacilli and the bacilli must then begin to die. When does this moment occur? In other words, *"When does the challenge begin and end?"*

It is at 50%—or halfway through the battle—that *'we meet the challenge.'* This, for the bacilli, is when the sugar has been **half**-consumed. One more division of the bacillus and the bottle of sugar water will have been consumed. The cells will have reached beyond their capacity, at only 50%.

The bottle of water is like the Earth. The people of the Earth (the bacillus) are busy working to raise the GDP (Gross Domestic Product) and to divide, grow, and consume even more. But, in fact, the real challenge has been overlooked in the process. The challenge is in maintaining sustainability of the Earth itself (the water with sugar). How do we move to sustainability?

Chapter 9

Life's Great Gifts: Courage and Determination

I did not build this boat to stay inside the harbor.

—Rumi

Frame Your Strongest Identity

As you build the story, it doesn't matter if the name is not your own in the telling. Each story always presents itself as everyone's life, each character as every man. We find parts of ourselves in the hero, no matter the name. The scenario is always, naturally, a part of our life unfolding anew. We settle in and listen—about ourselves.

For this reason, strongly fill each story with your own quest and your own self-discovery. Describing the challenge of identity reconstruction is a powerful use of any metaphor. We need to deeply associate with the person whose life is unfolding to the listener.

The process of seeking to define our individual *strongest identity* is much easier if we work from a framework of *questions for self-discovery*. In contemplating the answers to these questions, we begin a path towards clarifying the deep structure within ourselves. We must become clear on what in life supports our purpose and how to move past any parts of our old identity habits that may be limiting our evolution. This process creates advanced practice with a stronger self-identity. The metaphor is actually for ourselves.

What are the questions we can ask about ourselves that are fundamentals to our story?

At the basic integrity level of exploration, we need to ask ourselves:

1) **Who** am I?
2) **What** are my strengths?
3) **What** is my primary purpose in life?

These fundamental questions need depth probes. As we describe our character, we find more. Our voice, our gestures now hold this life powerfully, and the listener is also compelled to explore with us. Once you explore the basics, you can begin to probe deeper.

What if the first answer you get is just a simple doorway you go through to the next level of your life design? If your life was a tree, you could explore the roots of it, its basic thrust upward, and what allows it to flower. All of this allows your story to become fragrant with your own blossoming. Ask yourself the following questions and deeply contemplate the answers:

The Whys
- Why did I choose this particular direction?
- Why do I want to change or develop?
- Why it is worthwhile to evolve in this manner?

The Hows
- How do I find and develop my life's direction?
- How do I want to evolve in order to optimize who I wish to become?
- How can I perceive my mission in life or explore my vision?
- How can I take responsible roles effectively and mentor others to do the same?
- How can I learn to make the right choices to optimize what I have learned?
- How do I continue to optimize who I am becoming?
- How do I expand my ongoing sense of self?
- How do I develop my sensory awareness and my experience of presence?

The Whats
- What will allow me to best incorporate new dimensions of being?
- What will enable me to bring more passion into my life's work?
- What would help me dissolve older identities and drop them if they hinder progress?

These action steps then naturally follow:
- Managing boundaries between self and others.
- Learning how to say "no" to others when necessary.
- Learning how to ask for help when it is needed.

All these questions can unfold in the life and events of our story character.

The Story of Karl Wallenda

The story of Karl Wallenda is a fascinating tale. What would it mean to you to have your deepest joy—your skill and focus for mastery—also become completely linked to your deepest pain? Would you stop doing what you love? Or, would you move through it and obtain mastery? Karl Wallenda was a master who continued to develop mastery even in his darkest hour. However, he took time to reinvent the game of inner mastery such that it once again brought deep joy back into his life.

Some of you may have read the novelette about Karl and his five children, all tightrope walkers, working together in an amazing pyramid performance. They could be seen on 1950s' television shows such as the great Ed Sullivan Show, watched by millions on Sunday evenings. The pyramid was comprised of all six family members in total: three on the wire, two on the shoulders, and one on top of all the others. Quite an act!

Then, one day, for reasons unknown, all fell six stories to the ground. Two were killed. Two were badly injured, including Karl. The days of the wire-walking family ended in one moment.

My experience of Karl on the wire is very vivid because I saw him in person one time as a child. I went to a three-ring circus with my father and we sat in the bleachers. It was a fabulous experience for a 7-year-old: clowns in one ring mugging, tripping, pushing each other over, and pulling endless scarves out of their pockets; in the second ring, prancing ponies, with pretty girls in tutus standing on their backs; and, in the third ring were the lions and bears, and their tamers in red jackets, cracking whips while the animals jumped through hoops.

My father pointed to a high wire far above all the commotion. "See that wire way up there," he said with enthusiasm. "At the end of the show, a man will walk on that wire."

I still hear the sound of his name being announced and remember the figure below in a black, sequined outfit bowing to the crowd and quickly climbing the ladder up to the roof of the building. I remember the way he lovingly picked up the balance beam, set his posture, head up, and looked straight ahead, while he stepped out on the wire. And then, slowly and gracefully, high above all of us, and with no net, he danced on that wire!

What did Karl do after his terrible accident? How did he return to being the amazing wire artist that I witnessed?

After he fell with his family, he had major breaks all over his body. It took him six months to move, even with crutches. As soon as he was walking, however, he placed a wire two inches above the grass in his private backyard. There, every day, he practiced. Gradually, he moved the wire higher and higher. When reporters expressed amazement that he was planning to go back to the circus, he simply replied: **"Life is the wire. All the rest is waiting."**

Karl was a master. Amazing and powerful displays were practiced and mastered on that simple wire in the backyard of his home.

All alone on the wire, Karl mastered his own mind. He moved past fear through wire dancing. Each dance was different. Each filled with new expression. To the questioning reporters, he only replied again and again: **"Life is the wire. All the rest is waiting!"** Daily, he would move up the ladder to begin another expression of man-in-motion poetry.

A master aligns with his destiny. He knows his own resolve to be his deep choice and doesn't need the approval of society to make his choice. He lets his own vision choose his course and resolves to complete what he has begun.

What is your wire to walk on? What is your heart's desire? What destiny are you creating?

How does one walk a tightrope? The process seems simple and yet it deeply symbolizes all real mastery:

- First, one needs to deeply **focus on the value** and decide that it is worth it! One needs to commit!
- Then, one needs to find your inner **balance beam**. Balance is the essential ingredient of wire-walking mastery. It is also an essential ingredient in **all** mastery!

> - One also needs a **clear vision**. One needs to look 'way out' into the vision of effective results and see the way destiny beckons to **you**.
> - Finally, one needs to deeply **enjoy the moment!** Mastery means that we truly take time to dance!
>
> Remember Karl's heartfelt words: **"Life is the wire. All the rest is waiting!"**

Self-Mastery Coaching Through the Metaphor Story

We can ask coaching questions towards mastery in any story. While listening to the storyline, we and our listeners receive the widened overview and *coach position* awareness. They hear the open-ended questions in the story and then naturally ask the open-ended questions about themselves. Because the story is about someone else, they obtain a relaxed *observer's perspective* from which to explore their own questions.

The context sets them free to begin their own depth probe, even beyond rule structures that might guard against inner exploration. The story sets them on their path again, and they continue the most precious part of their journey.

To choose the best metaphor, you must seek to determine the key challenges of your listeners while, at the same time, noticing both the similarities and the unique aspects throughout the group you are addressing. Then invite a vision to form—a vision which includes higher integrity and unfolding awareness. Finally, select a story using your own intuition. Open to your vision and speak your story with benevolence and truth, embellishing the narrative with whatever nuances you may instinctively feel appropriate.

If possible, you can also demonstrate the process of self-coaching inside the metaphor. This is useful as a valuable expansion system for you, enabling your own development of congruence, self-awareness, and positive self-evaluation. Perhaps you will find some illuminating humor in your story that illustrates how a person becomes liberated from old, small-minded beliefs and behaviors.

CHAPTER 9 ❀ LIFE'S GREATEST GIFTS: COURAGE AND DETERMINATION   107

There is always a larger integrity you face towards in your story. You experience the unfolding search towards mastery as you speak. There is always a deeper capacity for truth and love that your story is finding. If you give yourselves to the story's search, you learn the story's lessons—with the listener.

Through your story, you can shine a beacon on the process of **self-mastery**. It is an exciting process: to teach the steps of widened self-awareness and witness the person or group begin to listen and deepen their own exploration and discovery, as you do so with yourself as well.

Coyotes in the Superstition Mountains

What has been your life's scariest experience so far?

I have never been afraid of starting out on an exploratory venture into the country wilderness. When I was an 8-year-old girl, I loved to walk out miles into the hills near the central California town where my parents lived, and visit the shepherds and their flocks. Since childhood, I have found the opportunity to wander off into the hills to be a great, sweet freedom.

I took this opportunity several times when I lived in Phoenix, Arizona, in my early thirties. Close to my home laid the vast wilderness of the Superstition Mountains, a range of mountains that is comprised of amazing rock formations, strange cactuses and plants, hidden springs, hundreds of trails, and rich wildlife.

Starting out on a five-day hike one early spring day, I first revisited beautiful areas that I had been to before. Several days later, I went over a range of high hills to find myself in a territory that seemed completely wild and desolate. Entering a small valley of scrub trees and bushes, I became aware that there were a great many animal prints in the dried soil. Walking down the trail, I saw more and more prints, and they all seemed to be different. Since I carried neither tent, nor weapon, nor matches, I sat down to drink some juice and consider the situation. The sun began to set.

The beautiful wild valley was very, very quiet, and I considered my options. One possibility was to turn back up the trail and into the hills again. I knew, however, that I had just spent an hour on the trail, crossing a very rocky and windy highland. To turn back now, as darkness descended, would neither provide safety nor a restful solution. It would be a long climb back to leave this quiet valley. It had been a long day and it seemed so easy to pull out my sleeping bag and lie down to sleep in the valley of footprints.

I vividly remember the moment, sitting there, asking myself to focus while pondering the alternatives. The best 'spot' to stay overnight in the valley didn't seem clear to me, as there were dried footprints everywhere, in puzzling array. Which animals? What to do?

Suddenly I saw him. It looked like a grey dog, watching me from the side of a nearby hill. I realized it was a coyote. He was sitting quietly, very relaxed, on his haunches, and observing me with interest. I nodded respectfully to him: "Hello Mr. Coyote, I'm just visiting. Please leave me alone" Then, without looking back, he trotted over the hill and out of sight.

"No problem here," I thought, "one interested coyote." But the vast array of footprints held my gaze. Many different animals had been here: an animal convention center.

The idea came like a flash. As a girl, I had read about the territorial practices of wolves in *Never Cry Wolf*, a biography by the famous naturalist Farley Mowat. He described how wolves in the Canadian north always respected the boundaries of his camp if he 'peed the borders' of his territory.

Focus turned into intention, and I thought to myself, "What a good idea! Let's test it." I spent at least an hour consuming enough liquid to do the job and sorting out my best boundary spots. I made them rather close, given the amount of liquid required. I carefully measured and marked, laughing to myself. I then lay down to sleep.

I would love to tell you that I had a quiet night. Not on your life! It was, in fact, the scariest night of my life. I woke up to see a vast array of stars in the pitch-black darkness and to hear the bush crashing and crunching with growling animals. All around me, there was an orchestra of grunts, barks, yelps, and mysterious noises. It was the national convention of coyotes in this small valley and, for sure, I was the prize exhibit. One group of animals would howl from one side of the valley and then come to visit close at hand. The howls would be picked up with barks on all sides. Again and again, I heard animals come and stir around my camp, though clearly none actually came past my borders. I lay there rather stiffly, shivering and praying, with only my nose poking out from my sleeping bag.

Finally, the noise stopped and dawn came. I peeked out. It had not been my best night of sleep. I arose, thankful and alert. The morning had brought me safety, and I could now dust myself off and see the new day. I was a 'city slicker in the wilderness,' yet the power of focused attention had allowed me to communicate to this wild pack and be respected.

Today, the story sometimes seems like a joke, but I use it to remind myself that the capacity to find good ideas when you need them is far from a joke. Our creative capacity to solve emerging problems in surprising ways is what defines us as being human.

My first thought was: "It was just a small idea from a book I read 20 years earlier." Since then, I have honored the creative flash much more. My inner guide assisted me when I needed it most on that spring evening in the hidden valley.

I read the Farley Mowat book when I was 10 years old. After 20 years of new input, the story was long buried, yet my inner request allowed me to recall exactly the 'best idea' for the moment. It was amazing that the old story and its solution-focused idea 'landed between my ears' when I focused and asked inwardly for help many years later.

Ask, ponder, and listen. Since then, this event has assisted me to build strong faith in the learning power of all of us. It has reminded me that all of us can find the critical solutions we need when we ask for them. **The inner guide emerges to assist!**

This capacity continually renews my faith in humanity. All of us, both alone and together, are capable of inner focus and leadership in the most critical moments. Is there some area, like a small valley, that you are in right now? Where do you need an inner assistant? **The inner guide will assist you!**

What is your valley? Your valley of paw prints to face? What do you need to do to face it well? **The inner guide will assist you!**

In the world as a whole, we are in a dark valley 'full of paw prints,' are we not? We see signs of danger all around, yet can barely understand the action steps needed to respond. Yet we can find the solutions that will bring our humanity through the dark times and into the fullness of our human powers. **The inner guide will assist us to find and take the best action steps... if we ask!**

Living in a World Full of Criticism

A particular story that was related to me years ago illustrates the powerful qualities of personal self-awareness, congruence, and internal self-consistency that Dr. Milton Erickson was known for. In the early 1950s, at a convention of physicians in New York City, the famous doctor planned a very standard demonstration of hypnosis that could prove useful for doctors. Since the convention took place at a medical hospital, the coordinators asked him to find a nurse there, who would be willing to be the demonstration subject. While checking through the halls, Milton met a young nurse named Cindy and, after a brief conversation, she agreed to be the subject.

The demonstration was planned for the afternoon. During the lunch hour, Milton remarked to the organizers that the demonstration subject would be the young nurse Cindy.

"You can't use her!" they all exclaimed. "Her friends have told us that she is suicidal. She is planning to quit work in two days and says she plans to end her life. Her friends are very worried about her, as are we. If you use her as a demonstration subject, this could make matters worse." Milton responded, "I suspect otherwise. She is excited about this now. If I don't use her as a demonstration subject, she is far more likely to have a negative response."

As the afternoon program began, Cindy proved to be a willing subject. Milton was quickly able to show the hypnosis features he had planned for his demonstration. With plenty of time to spare, he asked Cindy about some of her favorite places in New York City. She answered, "The botanical gardens, the zoo, and Coney Island." To which Milton replied, "Then let us take a small tour."

Inviting Cindy to do a detailed visualization, he had her inwardly tour some of her favorite pathways in the botanical gardens. With pleasure, she described a path of multi-colored dahlias and purple forget-me-nots, and banks of flowers of different sizes and shapes. She continued describing many areas, marveling at the trees from around the world, including the tiny bonsai trees.

Next, Milton assisted Cindy to visualize a trip to the zoo. Again, she enjoyed visualizing the different kinds of animals from various continents and how strange some of them were. She mentioned the baby ones and Milton had her linger to watch a mother monkey with her newborn, and then a baby rhinoceros, shyly peeking out from behind the legs of his giant, protective mother.

Finally, Milton took Cindy on a tour of the harbor where, through her visualization, she walked past all the cargo ships docking and unloading, and finally out to Coney Island where she observed picnicking families, children making sand castles on the beach, and young lovers strolling along the waterfront.

When he was finished, Milton thanked Cindy, said goodbye, and then left. One week later, he received a phone call in his Arizona home. "Cindy has disappeared," said the organizers of the conference. People had gone to her former apartment and found the apartment completely empty. Her friends told them that she was an orphan with no family, and they had no leads as to where she might have gone. Based on her former declarations, they believed she might now be dead, "And you may have killed her," they added. "Oh, I'm sure she will show up," said Milton.

One month later, still no sign of Cindy.

One year later, still no sign of Cindy. At the physicians conference, Milton noticed he was shunned.

Three years later, still no sign of Cindy. Milton continued to be treated as a pariah by the doctors at the convention.

Six years later, still no sign of Cindy. Now the topic was completely closed; people had forgotten about Cindy… but not Milton.

Twelve years later, Milton received a phone call at his Phoenix home. A woman's voice on the other end of the line said, "You probably won't remember me, but my name is Cindy and I was your demonstration subject twelve years ago at a conference of physicians in New York City." "Oh, I remember you well enough!" said Milton. "Where have you been?"

"I have just returned from Australia, where I now live with my family, my husband, and my three children," said Cindy. "After your demonstration 12 years ago, I was very moved and happy, so I went for a walk along the harbor. I met a young officer from a freighter bound for Australia the next day, and he mentioned that they badly needed a nurse onboard. I was leaving my job and apartment to make a change, and on the spur of the moment decided to join the boat. I gathered my passport and the things I needed, and left. Onboard, I met my future husband, an Australian, and we started our new life together in Australia. I'm here for a short visit, just to talk with old friends, and several of them mentioned I should call you.

"I knew you were okay," said Milton. "It's great to have something be completed well!!"

Self-Design Questions

With coaching and self-coaching frameworks in the story, we ask important 'self-design' questions which allow our listeners and ourselves to move deeper within the textures of their lives.

As we trust the process of finding our own inner truth, we learn to:
- evaluate older identities and discard them if they are irrelevant
- optimize who we are becoming
- explore our bigger vision
- perceive our mission
- take on expanded life dreams, and move beyond the challenges
- sponsor others to take their own learning steps to face their own challenges
- become as flexible as the situation requires and model that flexibility and self-trust through our stories

As the story unfolds, it is gratifying to demonstrate our hero's fortitude! It is valuable to detail how learning is being discovered and how the hero of the story determines his or her key risks, challenges, and choices. We discover the next steps and climb towards our purpose, associating with this hero, and our voice and body show the unfolding capacities.

Through careful descriptions, we demonstrate with body and tone all these emergent positive qualities. In this way, we truly show the nature of:
- coach position and the overview of value connection that it brings
- the surprises, unique challenges, disappointments, and difficulties
- the inner experience of discovering a wider system of awareness
- the renewed intention to produce inner development and enriched life

Becoming Cleopatra for the Crisis: Flexibility Coaching

Hearing about all the various financial crises in the world has me noticing the nature of fear. It is not really relevant whether you feel it or not. What is relevant is whether it stops you from doing what is required. How do you jump to your next level of flexibility if you feel fear?

Financial fears are interesting. What can allow us to weather any financial storm and learn from it? Pondering this, I remembered studying psychology in California in my mid-twenties. It was a financial crisis for me.

My education was expensive but important to me; I had moved to California with my two children for this purpose. I had arranged a suitable job as a clinical psychologist, but arrived to find the job had vanished with administrative changes. I could not afford to live in California. I had to shift perspective quickly to be able to stay. What a stretch! I pondered the newspapers and saw few opportunities. It was time to shift gears, and the prospect was scary.

I began to wonder how to become an entrepreneur, quickly. I decided I could make money with a series of evening 'Cooking Classes' for grade school kids in West Hollywood homes. This worked well for a group of 6- to 8-year-olds. Once a week, I gathered the young crew and we made pasta or fruit salad. I started organic vegetable gardens as well. (It was spring.) Great fun!

However, what I earned was just pocket change to pay the rent. Once again, many days of studying 'suitable' want ads proved discouraging until I went wild and became flexible. I found an agency that hired models to pose nude for regional art schools. Certainly not my normal 'self image,' but still enabling me to pay the rent while I went to school in the evenings. I soon found myself driving daily all over the greater Los Angeles area to one junior college or another.

CHAPTER 9 🌸 LIFE'S GREATEST GIFTS: COURAGE AND DETERMINATION

Picture the scene. It was rather disconcerting to arrive off a complex freeway exit, find parking, negotiate crowds of students and winding passages, and sprint into a college room full of people you have never met, only to immediately throw off all your clothing and pose 'naked as a jaybird.' Yet, the job paid well, and I could often read an interesting book while reclining like Cleopatra on a sofa, as an art class busily sculpted for three hours. Crisis resolved.

The key was flexibility. How do we find improbable ways to do what we want despite the odds?

If you are a corporate coach and your regular corporate clientele say they cannot currently afford the luxury of a personal coach, consider other variations: group coaching, team coaching, retirement coaching, job change coaching, or 'stress management' coaching. Consider incentives and special offers. **It is values, not dollars, which connect us!**

Emphasize measurement tools so managers can measure the value. Consider calling what you do by a different name. Even silly labels like 'Magicians Helper to Entrepreneurs: You get results or you don't pay.' Consider going into professional areas where jobs always tend to remain stable, such as government or education. Consider focusing on medical hospitals and health professionals. **It is values, not dollars, which connect us!**

Expand your vision! Find other strong niches, as well as your current area, and one of them may eventually be the one you keep. 'Flexibility Coaching' means being playful and giving lots of extras. It may mean adding some low cost or free exchanges. You learn to propose services that matter to people. Meanwhile, you are building relevant contacts.

It is values, not dollars, which connect us! *Our long-term vision brings energy when and where it counts. We find ourselves learning to relax even as we find different opportunities and markets that we didn't expect. Enjoy surviving your own particular 'crisis'! Then emerge and assist others with theirs.*

Designing Deep Renewal

With our story, we show a person at work evaluating and creating their more truthful awareness. If possible, you may want to demonstrate a big step in courageous self-realization: presenting the first steps that will determine their new beginnings.

We human beings spend our whole lives designing an effective identity. With any story we tell, it is valuable to clearly indicate all shifts towards deep renewal. For example, we can use a story to show the progress of a person who is courageously moving forward in a difficult situation. We can show them emerging in their commitment, moving beyond all stops along the way. We can show the person in the story creating their next level of integrity, truth, and mastery.

Our listeners always gain value if we show the context and if we demonstrate the holistic field of consciousness that moves our hero inexorably towards their own deeper self-knowledge. We want to celebrate someone as they are discovering a more courageous way of being.

Learning How To Walk

Milton Erickson used to tell a powerful story about his first days after becoming ill with polio as a boy. He discussed the inspiring idea he conceived that changed his life in a very positive way. Being ill became a springboard to some of his greatest questions and lessons.

Imagine being a 15-year-old boy who went to bed one evening with a sore throat and woke up three days later after nearly dying from polio. What would it be like for you if you discovered you could only move your eyes—that you were, in fact, paralyzed? That is the situation Milton experienced and lived through as a young man.

In the 1930s, medical authorities in rural areas of the United States didn't know what to do with a very ill boy like Milton. They simply helped his mother make a bed in the kitchen so he could be

CHAPTER 9 ❖ LIFE'S GREATEST GIFTS: COURAGE AND DETERMINATION 117

near her as she worked. There he lay, day after day, watching his mother at her daily tasks and busy with a newborn baby and a toddler.

Milton wished desperately to be able to move, and longingly watched and observed his newborn sister raising her head and lowering it. Because of his deep desire to regain his own mobility, he began to imagine himself being able to do that simple move and, surprisingly, after a few visualizations, he experienced some faint sign of movement in his neck muscles. With glee, he visualized again and again, and got more movement.

He realized he was on to something: he discovered he now had a path. He could do it. He began a daily routine, hour after hour, observing his baby sister and becoming familiar with her movements. He kept doing exactly what he saw her do in his mind's eye. Gradually, he regained muscle movement for himself. He learned to **do what it takes**.

Month after month, he continued with this daily visualization. As the baby learned to raise her hands, kick her legs, and so on, he practiced her techniques mentally. Then, as his abilities to move his body increased, he practiced physically. This he found difficult but possible—with visualization.

Two years later, after rigorous visualization and step-by-step practice, Milton was able to walk by using two canes. The doctors considered it a miracle; he considered it hard work. He had learned to **do what it takes!**

According to current authorities, Milton had rebuilt his damaged nerve pathways by using new brain territory. Some equated his new abilities to what babies are able to do if they have experienced brain damage before the age of six months. Milton noticed that the process required asking himself key questions, while he visualized again and again. He stimulated motivation at every level of brain and body.

The result for Milton was twofold. He not only regained a large degree of his lost capability, but created the opportunity to deeply understand the power of awareness, observation, question-asking, purpose exploration, visualization, and rapport. These well-practiced understandings gradually allowed him first, to walk; then, to finish high *school; and later, to begin a highly successful and creative medical career. He had acquired robust capacities to observe, question, and follow inner cues—capacities that most people never develop over a lifetime. Only we can determine our new beginnings and do what it takes to create them. Develop the power of awareness!* **Do what it takes!**

Chapter 10

Teamwork and Transformation

We are all on the team.

—Marilyn Atkinson

Breakthrough on the Trans-Canada Highway: The Trucker and the Hitchhiker

It was the late 1970s and I had the amazing adventure of driving an old pickup truck, hauling a small house trailer from New York across Canada to Vancouver. Familiar only with cars and short trips, this was a very unusual kind of adventure for me. I set out determined to have an interesting and safe trip but, within seven hours of leaving Toronto, I found myself with dimming headlights on an isolated northern stretch of the Trans-Canada Highway. The evening was getting dark quickly and my truck was losing power. I was just starting to despair when I found a gas station truck stop (with many large trucks in the parking lot). I pulled into the lot and rolled to a safe stop as the engine died. The station was dark, so I went into my trailer to sleep.

The next morning, I awakened to find that my small truck's battery was completely dead. A burley, gray-bearded trucker from one of the huge double semis in the back lot sauntered over and peered under the hood. He asked me to hit the gas, to test my ignition. He shook his head. "Your alternator is gone," he said.

I sighed. It was Sunday morning in Ontario. There would be no mechanic at this isolated station for 24 hours.

"I'll tell you what," said the trucker. "Two hundred miles down the highway is my hometown, where I own a vehicle scrap yard. For sure, I will be able to find you a working alternator to replace this one. That's your best bet! I'll get you started and, if you stick behind me all the way, you will do fine. I'll get you your alternator and you just carry on with your journey."

What wonderful help! In a jiffy, the trucker had my engine running and we started down the road, me following a safe distance behind his huge truck.

Several hours later, I saw a young German hitchhiker. He was wearing unbelievable green lederhosen and a cap with a feather, and holding a big sign: "University student hitchhiking to Vancouver. Please help."

He looked friendly and cheerful. I pulled up, curious to see if he really was a German teenager wanting a ride. After three or four sentences, I was convinced. He told me that he had been stuck there for two hours.

I motioned him to the other side of the truck and reached over to open the door. My foot slipped off the gas, the engine stalled, and we were suddenly both stuck. Meanwhile, I saw the back of the trucker's huge, long-haul semi disappear over the far hill up ahead. Now, there were two of us stuck on the Trans-Canada Highway.

The hitchhiker and I got acquainted, and discussed our dismal options of assistance in this isolated location. I decided to make a cup of coffee in the trailer before taking any action. As I poured the coffee for the hitchhiker and myself, I heard a honk and saw the trucker with his giant semi, returning over the hill again to rescue me. He honked again and waved as his brakes squealed from the long hill.

As he pulled up to a screeching stop across the road from me, the shoulder of the road gave way and the back half of his huge vehicle suddenly slid down the bank and into a ditch. Now, there were three of us stuck on the Trans-Canada Highway.

Imagine this moment, which was well before the era of cell phones. The trucker surveyed the damage and shook his head. The big truck was almost on its side. I made a third cup of coffee and some sandwiches for him and the hitchhiker. None of us spoke much.

Then the rescue team arrived, all quite suddenly, and, for me, most unexpectedly. Each one was a trucker driving a long haul. They didn't realize they were the rescue team until they saw the truck in the ditch. Each stopped automatically with the aim of helping. Within ten minutes, six large semi-trailer trucks were stopped on the Trans-Canada Highway—four on one side, and two on the other. They followed the basic 'we all serve each other' agreement between truckers in distress. Now, with seven huge vehicles plus my own, we looked like a small town gathered together. The highway was now effectively blocked except for one lane.

Everyone went into action. The perfect team formed. It was a wonderful thing to watch individuals in a group discover that they are part of a team. The men all surveyed the problem, and huddled together. They checked the damage, discussed, and figured their options. One of them took the lead and assigned jobs. Everyone scurried for chains and other equipment.

As I watched, I saw that it was clearly not an easy operation. The truckers clamored around: pulling out lengths of chain, measuring and discussing. They huddled around one drawing an individual had made, showing ropes and pulleys, then threw it away and made another.

Meanwhile, the hitchhiker, in his green Lederhosen, was also working hard. He was now planted in the middle of the road, directing the single lanes of traffic from both directions through the blockage; first, motioning through a group of cars from the left and then, firmly stopping them and motioning another group of cars from the right. With his cap, feather, and green Lederhosen, he was a curious participant in the role, but the traffic obeyed his firm command.

I ran back and forth from the trailer, making coffee for the truckers. I made sandwiches too, but most of them were too busy to eat.

It took them an hour and a half of focused work, lining up trucks side by side to do the final operation. In one lurching, well-coordinated, three-truck pull-job the huge semi was removed safely from the ditch. They all cheered. Done, they slapped each other on the back, jumped into their rigs, and were off.

Now, the three of us—only the trucker, the hitchhiker, and I—remained. The trucker was elated and joyous over the smooth rescue. In a moment, he had my truck restarted and the hitchhiker finally had his ride. An hour later at his automotive yard, he assembled the new alternator for me. In an hour and a half, my truck was humming with its new working part and I was off, fully operative, to begin the next leg of my journey.

Notice the wonderful discoveries I made through this experience. I learned that people are heros at heart, simply waiting for opportunities to really draw out their heroism. I learned that people will happily become part of a team and pitch in fully when the need is clear. **When we are in trouble, the team appears. And, it does appear.** What's more, people come through at their best—giving from the heart, doing their heroism gladly. This is truly what it means to be human!

> *Have you also discovered this yourself? The stories we tell to each other are full of such natural moments of real heroism! They are not just about special people; they are about all of us. We have all experienced the team and it is us! We are the heros, the givers, or the partakers in the big game.* **We are already on the team!**

Pondering a Metaphor Into Life

The methodology of pondering a metaphor into life gives us a basic understanding of what life is all about. A strong metaphor reflects our sense of purpose. Ideas are only grasped fully when they reflect a corresponding inner development.

When listening to a metaphor story, we get an understanding of what exists within ourselves. When we carefully contemplate the similarities, we discover the depth of this understanding within our own psyche. Nothing exists in ourselves that we have not taken within, digested, and deeply considered—with much more than the mental apparatus that we may think we have. We are much bigger than the small stories we tell people about our personal lives. There is the metaphor, and then there is the deep question inside the metaphor. The thoughts that humans ponder are how we affirm our own experiences.

The conscious mind is driven to find answers about what instances could sabotage survival and therefore move a person towards **negative thinking**. Negatives multiply quickly into more negatives. The negative thought processes move people towards a life that is imprisoned by habits, a life that is tiresome and mundane—therefore mainly focused on adversity and misfortune.

In telling our story, we endeavor to demonstrate the important questions that lie within the action. Our story unfolds to show how a specific dilemma represents an important human concern. This important question shows up in the story about someone's life experience, and that question goes deeper than surface appearances—beyond what is normally noticed by the conscious mind.

What is the pearl inside the story that opens up to shine for us? The pearl of wisdom in your metaphor shows that in order to understand an idea, we must have actually put it to use somewhere and somehow. Through the story, we gradually become familiar with all its subtle ramifications and connections with other ideas already developed through previous experiences. We know much more than we think we do. Like our pearl, the metaphor will gradually take root and grow in us as a natural process because it reflects a truth we already know at a deeper level.

How Do We Build 100% Commitment?

Commitment provides a vortex for development because, like appreciation, it is not based on anything tangible. It is impactful to describe, in the story, the process of building commitment. For example, you might describe a person who gradually builds commitment with their daily actions. This will get the point across that, simply put: *If we commit 100%, we get a 100% result.*

What's remarkable is that 100% commitment is actually easy! Describe the process of an easy approach in your story. Show and detail how and when the *shift* takes place. Show that commitment is mainly a matter of clear and persistent declaration—both to self and to others. When we give ourselves 'self-reminders' of our commitment, our inner faith becomes stronger.

What does viewing and hearing about 100% commitment give us:
- We learn to link into the most empowering mission outside of the personal self.
- We learn to look beyond emotional concerns to a clear definition of our key principles.
- We learn to move beyond our doubts to the most revitalizing value states we can find—then we can declare these as the source of our motivation—especially love, compassion, and gratitude.
- We learn to set our intention on the strongest set of capabilities and build the necessary distinctions to make our vision happen.
- We learn to declare our commitment to personal well-being.
- We learn to declare consistency and a decision towards integrity.

- We then can declare that commitment is what our life is all about!
- We take a warm coach position on our connection to others and see our life, our values, and our actions benefiting everyone!

100% commitment is easy when we declare our willingness to reinstate our declaration whenever we break it. We are assisting others to do the same. To detail this growth—or any part of it—in your story is to truly give people faith that they too can muster 100% commitment.

This means an attitude of total self-forgiveness—the hard part! If you are willing to use your own difficulties with this in your story and show the process of building commitment through difficulties, your story now inspires the recommitment—and self-forgiveness—of your listeners.

Can We Follow the Track?

In 2000, on a cold winter afternoon in Kiev, I had finished training and was preparing to leave for Riga, Latvia, where I was scheduled to teach a class at 9:30 the next morning. Just before leaving for the airport, I learned that there had been an airline breakdown—my flight had been cancelled!

My Ukrainian hosts quickly determined that not only were there no other flights to Latvia, there was no other public transport to get me to Riga in time for the class.

The person who organized the course in Riga was frantic—she had 110 people waiting! I was told that it was possible to drive overnight from Kiev to Riga. After hurried discussions, long-distance calls, local calls, and hearing the entreaties of the Riga course organizer, I decided to make the 8-hour drive... via a mountainous highway through Belarus.

Hearing the urgency in my voice, my hosts made hurried inquiries to find a person who could get me there in time. They quickly found

Oleg: a stocky, bespectacled Ukrainian man, in his thirties, who was willing to drive me to Latvia. I went outside to inspect his vehicle. It was a grey-colored van in good repair. He showed me that he had extra tires, two tanks of gas, and food and blankets to take upon the journey. We negotiated a price and rushed to the Belarus offices to get our visas to cross Belarus. Then, the three of us: the driver, Sergei, a coaching student from Kiev, and I set out together.

It was 9:00 p.m. on a clear, starlit, mid-winter evening when we left Kiev. There was an eight-hour journey ahead, according to the best estimates from the map. "'No problem," we all thought. Our driver, Oleg, smiled and said, "It will be easy." There is a saying that we need to be prepared for the worst. No team can be totally ready. So Sergei and I started to visualize our journey, as Ukraine and Belarus driving conditions are always quite changeable.

We started full of anticipation and energy. We were ready and willing to tackle our overnight drive. We were ready even when the road headed steeply into the mountains. We were ready even when the rain started to pour down, mixed with ice crystals. We were ready when the road moved from pavement to gravel, and we traveled high into terrain where there were seldom any cars or trucks. We were even ready when the sleet turned to snow, and when the snow became a blizzard. We were still ready when the sky got so dark with blowing snow that we could not see the road at all. It all happened rather fast.

The changes in the conditions were so precipitous that, suddenly, we found ourselves with zero visibility on a high mountain road with the road disappearing beneath the snow. There was no other traffic anywhere. We were suddenly alone in a howling mountain blizzard. We began to wonder if we were really ready for **this!**

The driver was following the slightest trace of the blurred track ahead of us, moving at five miles an hour. Earlier, Oleg had been very talkative but now he said nothing. He hunched over the steering wheel with his face close to the windshield, straining to see the road. The windshield wipers couldn't keep the windshield clear. The tire tracks from earlier cars had disappeared. We couldn't see much at all. Sergei was watching from the window, and assisting with 'edge of the road' reports. I, the non-Russian speaker, kept quiet in the back seat.

> *The driver Oleg suddenly lurched to a halt. It was as if we were driving into a wall of snow. No one said anything for five minutes. The decision to surrender was clearly in the air. Could we even move forward at five miles per hour?*
>
> *Suddenly, the blizzard diminished. It was a surprise. Just like that, as fast as it had begun, the snowfall was complete. The road became barely visible. The snow was about nine inches high.*
>
> *The Ukrainian driver started to move the van slowly. At the same time, he began to whistle a small lilting tune. Sergei started to keep time with a clap. I joined in with a small counter beat and started to hum. In five minutes, we were all enjoying the fun and singing loudly, as the van moved at fifteen miles per hour. And we were having fun! Our aim to take care of each other was now blessed with simple joy in the moment. Soon we sang and howled with glee, as if the outrageous singing totally realigned and counterbalanced our former fears. Two hours later, we came down from the mountains and met a plowed road. Our journey, once again, opened up before us.*
>
> *I arrived in Riga the next day, tired, relieved, and a little late, to a standing ovation from the waiting students. I thanked Oleg for his skill, patience, endurance, and a lesson in teamwork.*

Life's Companions: A Short Exercise

Life is a journey—and on this journey you will have companions. These companions are very important to you and help you towards discovering your life's meaning.

Think about the key companions on your own personal journey?

- Select 10 people who are truly important players in your life.
- View them in your mind's eye. See them pass before you—one by one.
- Honor each one of them as they pass.
- See their beauty, their strength, their wisdom, and their courage.
- Say a word or two to each of them as they pass before you in your mind's eye.

- Gather them as energy, and feel the energy of their presence in your heart.

Now, allow a simple story to come to mind that you want to tell—a story meant only for these companions! Let the story develop organically in your mind; it does not have to be a good story or even the right story. Do not try to change or edit it or explain it.

In your mind's eye, begin to tell your story to them, and let the tones of your story evoke the powerful energies that you and each of your companions share. Let the tones evoke the deep truths, the wonderful mysteries of life that you and your companions experience together in life's special moments. As if it were a song, let the tones also evoke your commitment to your these people. Let the tones of your story carry the deep energies of love and warmth that you enjoy with them!

Now go and tell your story. Do not let the moment pass. Find at least one of these people and share your illumination with them.

Getting Over the Fence

One time, on the Island of Cyprus, I worked with a special purpose team, taking a three-day tour together as they organized a difficult project. This team was a group of people who had just formed their team about three or four days earlier, and were still scraping around in the 'brainstorming' phase (trying to work out leadership). As well, they were somewhat apprehensive about the task in front of them, a big task. They had taken on a project to build a sports facility, and they were exploring the specifics—multiple complex steps. Funding was a big project, and they were working through the financial challenges. The team included people with various different generic abilities: some engineers, some managers, a town planner, and an architect.

We took an afternoon with the team, and went out to visit an ancient Roman city on an old country road, a long drive from the city of Paphos, only to find, on arrival, that the main gate was closed. We noticed that there was an open gate three miles away, but that was too far from our road. It was a hot day and nobody wanted to walk three miles around the fence to the other gate. We stood and discussed, disappointed that our planned outing had been stopped.

Meanwhile, one engineer discovered that, in one spot, it was possible to hoist himself over the very high fence. He was a very athletic young guy, and he managed to climb to the other side thinking he could open the gate. In fact, he couldn't. He was on one side; we were on the other.

His next intention was to assist all nine of us to follow his climb. It was quite the escapade for ten people: using feet, hands, boosting, and lots of laughter. Each of us was a different age and some of us wore skirts, so the small team had to treat each individual as a special project. We strategized who would go first, receiving lots of hooting and encouragement. We gradually worked out who would go last, using everyone's muscle and know-how. None of the rest of us were athletes, but our leader continually encouraged us 'from the top,' taking all the care required for each person, step by step, to follow him 'way up and over.' The fence had barbed wire at the top. Can you imagine?

We all made it over the fence with each other's help. For each person, we worked together as a team, protecting clothes from the barbed wire. We were assisting each other personally, safely up and safely down. As each person made it, we hooted and hollered. One by one, we got over the fence.

That day, we became 'The team that went over the fence!' On the spot, the team had an identity and a track record: we were the team who could help each other and laugh together! We were the Fence Climbers, and so, necessarily, also capable of succeeding with the other aspects of the difficult project! In the moment of taking action together, a team finds its true team identity.

Team Humanity—Getting Over The Fence

The giant team called **Humanity** is stuck with each other in today's world—on the wrong side of the fence. The fence is our capability to handle solutions for the difficulties we all jointly share. **Team Humanity** needs warmth, humor, and the willingness to join together to find unique solutions to get us all *over the fence*. The fence has many facets:

- physical (planetary)
- relational (international agreements)
- creative (general sharing of education and joint resources)
- meaning (willingness to find best choices)

A Story Called "Failing Forward"

If something is worth doing, it is worth doing badly at the beginning. We often need to practice again and again—and this is natural. We need to be willing to make mistakes—the first time, the second time, and however many times it takes. In this way, we learn to reinstate our commitment over and over without any predilections of self-defeat. The meaning of *failing forward* is forgiving our *mis-takes*. We might 'miss the first take,' but we always get another shot.

Winston Churchill once said, "Success is having failure after failure with no loss of enthusiasm!" The same is true for all humanity. Evolution is forever a work in progress. No vision is ever a done thing no matter how many 'takes' it takes to build a clear next step. As long as we continue to be inspired by the visions and efforts of all humanity, we are evolving in our capacity to evolve!

Chapter 11

Friendship and Love

When the smoke-and-mirrors ego surrenders to Vastness, There's nothing left but **holy holy holy!**

—*Rumi*

Link People to Deep Principles

When you are telling a story, use metaphors to link people to deep principles that naturally expand consciousness. We step into the principles, like shoes, and walk towards our purpose. Speak these principles with strong tonal emphasis while telling the story. A principle provides a powerful way to reconnect to inner purpose!

Punch holes in people's cynicism with your stories! For example, if they think they are unlovable, help them to discard these old beliefs like tattered rags by showing how love renews itself. Then, link to a powerful principle of love's invincibility: *Love is for the finding! We can always find love again!*

If someone is convinced that he or she has been damaged from an experience that happened earlier in his or her life, you can illustrate a story of someone with a difficult childhood who is now doing exceptionally well! Then you can add a strong punch line at the end such as: *We can always build a great relationship!*

Through your story, you can encourage a person or group to "*try on*" clear principles. Your principles should appear in the story as an emerging discovery system for both your listeners and the hero of the story.

Develop a story that creates a vision of transformational abilities emerging from transformed principles. Whenever possible, describe the chain of events as if it was a film or *motion picture* with strong repeating descriptive phrases. Multiple perceptual positions can make your principles come alive while the story becomes rich in detail! Expansion into the future creates an overarching experience of natural recommitment.

For example, what stories might you build to express the following two ideas?

- People respect you when you speak out for and about your commitments.
- You can maintain your power while still being open to receive from others.

Metaphors can build inner principles that respond like seeds in good soil—they immediately start to grow in people's lives! Your seeds of visionary possibility find the *rich soil of real inquiry*. The listener is refreshed and begins to put down new roots of curiosity about life. These roots will soon germinate, sprout, and flower into the clear distinctions and refined abilities needed to deeply focus on their life's goals.

Esref, the Blind Painter… the Flow of Vision

Coaching is all about the rise of insight, whether it comes slowly or in a flash. Inner vision allows us to see a sparkling idea, follow a brilliant guiding plan, and advance towards a glowing future.

Notice the words in the above paragraph. In all languages, words of brightness and of sight dominate all accounts of inspiration. When we see the power of visualization as illuminating the pathway to all true inspiration, the world of inner knowing begins to open before us. 'Insight' has deep meaning.

Real vision takes us beyond immediate perception, or ideas of past and future. It is unlimited. There is increasing evidence that inner vision does not depend on the body's eyes at all. The mind is a vehicle for vision, and the source of true vision.

I recently watched a video of Esref, a citizen of Ankara, Turkey, a man with no eyes. Blind his entire life, he paints amazing pictures. This man, who crafts with color and perspective, envisions with his hands by using deep intention to 'see' and create beauty. What flows from his thoughts is the clarity that beautiful dreams are made of. Call it the vision of 'inside vision'! **His teaching and his request to those around him is this: Know that you, also, can find your own inner vision!**

His face glows with joy as he creates. He uses his fingers with the precision of a man who truly realizes what is important in the shaping of a dream. As I watched him lay down colors, I remembered Helen Keller's words: "People pity me that I cannot see or hear. Far worse is a life without vision!" **Find your own inner vision! Develop that!**

> *Esref's paintings are remarkable, but even more so is the man himself, deeply engaged in giving the world his true gift. To see him work is to reflect on the amazing flow of human potential to unfold our inner transformational awareness by opening vision.*
>
> *What does this evidence say to us as solution-focused coaches? To me, it is a reminder of the fire of awakened insight available at all times to everyone we coach. It is a reminder to each of us to refrain from negative conclusions about any single person. Instead, notice their journey towards insight… and how to assist them. In Milton's words: "People are okay and they have the resources they need." They can find their own insight as we coach them.* **Find your own inner vision! Develop that!**

Create With Principles and Punch Lines

Use your metaphor to acknowledge or demonstrate one specific guiding principle. *If you do one at a time and only one per story*, it allows the principle to resonate so that the listeners really ponder it.

Basic ideas like *"create clear boundaries"* or *"forgiveness is the best policy"* are simple guiding principles which you can activate and develop, bringing people alive to the deeper essence. We assist our listeners to ponder and become observers to their own examples. They re-explore their own thoughts and habitual beliefs from another point of view. They realize that they are growing beyond the old idea and notice the self as fresh and new. They realize: *"I am more than the content of my conscious mind!"*

A great way to develop your story is to start with your principle. Choose the purpose that you want to serve through the story, otherwise known as the ***engaged meaning***, and signify it with your principle phrase—your main point or ***punch line***.

You could try an experiment right now: Think of a principle you want to extol, and empty your mind and wait for a story to come to mind that supports it. If you ask, it will come to you!

Punch Line Questions Call Us to the Quest

You can always deliver *punch line questions* inside your metaphor as well. With a particularly abstract idea, ask a punch line question to *bring home* the meaning. It can be an open question designed to stimulate scrutiny.

Examples of punch line questions:
- So how will you know if you have a real result?
- Where is love waiting for you this day?
- How will I discover my next step, even here?

Like the '*as-if*' frame in coaching, it works best if you present the question again at several other points—at least three times, inside the story. Repeat your guiding question or principle at least three times inside the story to generate sticking power.

In solution-focused communication, we are leaning in to a positive purpose, evoking images of holistic renewal. We are engaging vision! Our brain is designed for visualizations, and positive vision is always undeniable. With principles, questions, and engaged vision, our story becomes compelling imagery.

With the metaphorical imagery and feeling, we are also evoking energy. Any physicist will tell you that the whole universe—all of space, time, and matter—is just pure energy. We humans are powerful energy generators! This means that your story needs to evoke positive emotion to generate energy for **self-trust**.

For integrative learning to be effective, we need at least three exposures to the theme or three verbal presentations with tonal emphasis to mark out a key concept and make it stick in the mind. The same is true with your story and its deep principles!

Evoke your images in a manner that will stimulate people's imaginations. Speak powerfully and tonally! Link to vision, and remember to mention the principles at three key points throughout your story to solidify their resonance.

Trust your own vision and its own unfolding, and feel your deep principles. As the principles emerge, speak them with power! Speak them again and again and again and each time savor them. Feel the energy you emit as you tell your story. Your declaration is also—and always will be—for yourself, as well as those you inspire.

The Story of Jacob's Ladder:
Renew Your Energy!

The story of "Jacob's Ladder" is a powerful Christian myth. It relates to the biblical figure, Jacob, and his dream of a huge ladder extending to heaven, with angels ascending and descending on it. What do you see when you imagine that? The dream image of Jacob's ladder shows how to re-associate to one's commitment, no matter what.

The ladder represents some basic laws of self-development that are true for all of us. The idea might be presented as a series of discoveries. The first discovery is that everyone is able to climb alone for awhile, but if people only work for themselves the energy diminishes. This means that many people stop climbing, and find themselves suspended. **Assist others and find your own life energy!**

The people who are able to continue discover a key rule: you can climb to the next rung when you bring someone to the rung you've reached! Assist another and your motivational energy releases you to continue. **Assist others and find your own life energy!**

The final rule is that blessing and forgiveness release you. Forgive someone and you can climb! Honor their attempts and you can climb further. Bless others with compassionate awareness and you find great energy.

We are all climbing Jacob's ladder! If we warmly assist our companions, the way becomes easy. **Assist others and find your own life energy!**

In other words, you take the next step with your own inner growth when you bring someone else to the step you are on. You only reach enlightenment when you assist enlightenment. **Assist others and find your own life energy!**

Milton Erickson's Principles

Milton Erickson was a great American psychiatrist who shaped the beginnings of solution-focused methodology. He was a great storyteller throughout his entire career. He used his stories for healing, and showed a path towards transformational metaphors that provides powerful examples for all who followed after.

Milton Erickson emphasized basic principles in his stories. He emphasized that people always have the resources to develop themselves and that people are always 'okay.' In other words, people can always move out of the old, black, negative emotional systems into the light of self-awareness. In his stories, he showed that people have full access to the inner resources they need for self-growth… and can shift at any time.

He also emphasized the power and value of compassion for others, pointing out that all people do the best they can in any situation and are generally willing to progress further up the ladder towards attainment of their goals. The coach's role is to assist clients in developing familiarity with the wide range of their own capabilities, evoking the power of their values.

As Milton Erickson put it: *"Never despair; change is inevitable!"*

The next story is sourced from Milton and is an expression of these principles in action.

Milton and George

Milton Erickson often told stories about his work with patients in the mental hospitals where he had been employed as a young psychiatrist. He once described his experiences with a man named George, who, as he described it, spoke 'word salad,' a mixture of multiple, 'mixed up' phrases, nouns, and verbs in no clear order. Milton met George on his very first day in charge of the back wards at the Worcester State Mental Hospital in Massachusetts. Five years earlier, George was brought to the hospital from a back road where he had been wandering aimlessly. No one could discover his last name and background because he only spoke 'word salad.' Only his first name, George, identified him.

Milton's earliest preliminary meeting with George startled him. As Milton toured one back ward for the very first time, George, who had been sitting passively on a bench, suddenly jumped up, ran towards Milton, and, in an excited tone of voice while waving his arms, began to speak word salad, continuing for about two minutes! The nurses explained that he only did this when a new person came into the ward.

Milton listened with interest, went away, and returned with his secretary who knew shorthand. She notated George's words as Milton listened to George a second time. Then, Milton spent several weeks carefully developing a word salad of his own, and practicing it until he could say it by heart. **Deep connection takes commitment.**

When he was finally ready, Milton went to George's ward once again. George jumped up, came forward, and spoke three sentences of excited word salad. Milton responded right back with similar excitement and three sentences of his own word salad. George seemed astounded, and went and sat on the bench, eyeing Milton with interest. Milton also sat down, and waited.

It took him ten minutes of thought, but finally George stood up and paced up and down near Milton, speaking methodically in word salad. It was as if he was telling a reasonable story step by step. He spoke in word salad for ten minutes. When he was done, he went and sat on the bench. Now, Milton stood up and, for ten minutes, he paced up and down and responded with methodical, reasoned word salad. He then sat down on the bench.

Another round began: George stood up and, with many gestures and much more passion in his voice, started a monologue in word salad for half an hour. It was as if he was telling Milton his authentic feelings about life, yet only in word salad. Bringing himself totally into the conversation, he sometimes sounded sad, sometimes angry, and sometimes excited.

Milton listened carefully to the total expression, and when it was his turn, he spoke for a similar period and, like orchestral replay, he brought the entire emotional range into his voice as well. He sat down on the bench.

George, who had been calmly sitting on the bench, watching, and listening, nodded gravely as if in agreement. Now, George stood and spoke for 20 minutes in tones of sadness, his word salad full of emotion. **Deep connection takes commitment!**

Milton again matched in tempo, and he replied with warm tones, responding with gentle word salad to George's emotion.

Now, George reached towards Milton once again, "Speak sense, Doctor," said George. "I will," responded Milton. "Then tell me... what is your last name?"

George spoke two sentences of word salad and said his last name. Milton responded with two sentences of word salad and asked, "Where are you from?" Within an hour, Milton had extracted the basics of George's history.

Through weekly communication with Milton, George became a changed man. He had a friend. At first, he only talked with Milton but gradually over the next weeks and months, he made more and more understandable communications to others. Soon, he was out working on the grounds. The hospital learned that his family was dead, but that he had inherited a small farm. Executors had been looking for him. About eleven months after Milton's first talk with him, he was capable of returning to that farm.

He lived there for the rest of his life and, for 40 years, maintained yearly communication, by postcard, with Milton. His messages were cryptic: "Built a new roof on the barn this winter." Or, "15 new lambs, all in good shape." Then he would sign his name, "George," and finish with two sentences of word salad!

What does it mean to listen to someone? Do we only listen to the words, or can we listen to the heart? What does it mean to speak to someone? Can we only speak our reasoned thoughts, or can we speak our deep awareness? Only we can decide how far we reach across the gap to recognize and create connection with someone! **Deep connection takes commitment!**

Rites of Passage

Rites of passage frame some of Milton Erickson's great metaphoric themes. In his metaphors, he would often describe developmental stage learning by vividly describing a person in crisis and demonstrate that person accelerating past all stops into a stage of growth. As a storyteller, I have followed this example and found key moments from my own personal 'rites of passage.'

For example, my story about "The Teddy Bear's Picnic" is about a rite of passage—a demonstration of risk-taking ability.

People are deeply interested in the *'Rite of Passage'* theme because it describes the process of launching out towards new experiences even when you feel you are not ready. When we really check our own experience, we find that 'not ready' is the usual self-talk that people say to themselves. People never feel they are *ready* to jump to the next level of awareness because they are not yet clear that they are competent enough to take that next jump. These stories provide a valuable little push, the catalyst they need to trigger them to action.

You can also use jokes to illustrate how people dare to move forward. For example, I sometimes reference the story of the man who advertised an *"almost brand new Mercedes, driven only for six weeks during an identity crisis."* We can ask the question: How will we look back later at the learnings from those early stages? We need to celebrate the courage to move from the old stage to the new. Many stories in this book are designed to encourage this tenacity.

The important components of these metaphorical themes point out the key *mind shifts* that make forward movement possible. You describe a hero in a story giving up a negative old habit and focusing on life renewal and, as you detail it, your audience notices their own rites of passage. You create change by creating contrasts. For example, perhaps you detail the difference between early stage, vague *possibilities thinking* towards a goal, and the necessary *'procedural thinking'* which then develops real steps to make that goal actually come to fruition. Now your audience builds their own distinctions to notice what step they are on.

As you speak your story, you can create a voice tone shift that contrasts two key levels of awareness as the hero of the story shifts back and forth. The aim is to show the *'spring of re-engagement'* after a *'winter of discontent.'* The story describes how the transition is completed and the person moves forward.

Catching Planes:
The Wonder of Just in Time

We all drink from wells we did not dig!

'Just in time' thinking is a wonderful system the Universe has devised for grabbing our attention and directing it back into the salience of the moment: a moment of rich experience, warm hearts, love, gratitude, and wonderful people. We puncture and deflate our cynicism balloon, raise the flag of human heroism, and realize that we live in a world of truth, beauty, humor, and goodness!

One area that opens our hearts in a compelling way is the heroic 'friendship account' we can build with the strangers who we find in emerging moments of difficulty. Everyone I know can find several. Can you? Strangers offering friendship in difficult moments have filled my heart with enough joy for a lifetime. We all remember deep, warm-hearted help received when we needed it most. **Just in time come the friends!**

All of my life, I will remember my gratitude to a housewife who saw me, my husband, and my family stuck with a major car breakdown in central Mexico in 120°F heat. She walked out of her fine home, inquired about our well-being, invited us in, and gave us tall, cold drinks and snacks, while finding toys for our 3-year-old.

I was pregnant and experiencing major morning sickness. The support came at exactly the right moment. Suddenly, I was lifted by the hospitality of a stranger into the zone of compelling love and care for those in distress. **Just in time!**

Airports are another area! My life as a constant traveler, catching planes on a weekly basis, has been filled with the effort of an army of heros. One morning, missing the correct airport terminal in Singapore,

> a wonderful, rather tiny taxi driver grabbed my three large suitcases and hauled them past several barriers to get them into the boot of his cab. Upon hearing that I was late for my flight, he whipped through traffic for several miles, making U-turns and reverses, all with the laughing spirit of a champion. He delivered me to the right door of the right airport area—**just in time!**
>
> On another occasion, my husband, Lawrence, and I were quite lost in the huge Denver Airport complex, and were individually 'carted' for 10 miles by a friendly young woman. Seeing our emergency, she missed her lunch to take us on her 'trolley to a whole different airport.' We got to our plane—**just in time!**
>
> There was an occasion when, after a long drive, we arrived in Moscow during the morning rush hour and I realized that my flight would be leaving from an airport on the other side of the city. This meant it was still almost 100 miles away by the 'ring road.' The solution was difficult: cross Moscow by subway at rush hour! Several friends stood with me, elbow to elbow, on crowded subways, holding my huge bags. My friends hauled these large suitcases up and down the subway stairs. In this way, we scooted from one side of Moscow to the other. Once again, I caught my plane with moments to spare. **Just in time come the friends!**
>
> What does the universe do for you that makes you stop and count your blessings? A great coaching experience, a moment of friendly flow online, greeting friends you haven't seen for a while, or perhaps seeing your beloved after a journey? Allow gratitude to carry you through the dark winters of the soul and to open your heart... **just in time!**

Love Expands Beyond Emotion

Love, as a value, isn't emotion. Emotions go up and down. Love, as a value, is *stable*. It is true *devotion*, the expression of deep commitment and joyful awareness. In other words, love, as a value, speaks to the process of *discovering love*, no matter the context.

In some ways, this is the same as '*falling in love*.' Love is experienced as a sustainable capacity to share knowledge, to share energy, and to share each other's truth—yet it lacks all expectation. It is a realizable value. When we '*fall in love,*' we experience the awareness, presence, and wisdom of life.

Love can be described in a story in many ways. We can show the timeless, spacious, unhurried process of cherishing another person and of deeply honoring each moment shared together.

Our stories can show how a person may feel diminished for a spell of time and how the energy of love diminishes at the same time. The ego-identification cries out with expectations! If we don't resist the diminishment, however, then the space and power of life's energy below that emerges. We always feel this as joy and love for this next moment in our life. We stop our grasping and find our heart-connection. True value comes into awareness, and our deeper capacity for love as devotion emerges. Our stories can show how this happens.

Through transformational metaphors, we can learn to recognize the various '*closed rooms*' in our inner world so that we do not linger in them, but make haste outside the boundaries towards true self-discovery. When sufficient information has emerged—when larger patterns or relationships are perceived—a natural shift of perception spontaneously occurs! We see and hear again what is worthy of our love. How wonderful it is that great metaphors can provoke this so powerfully!

A metaphor becomes transformational when it shows people deeply at work, finding a doorway to a re-emergence that frees them. During the process of finding a source of love, people listen to the story, try on their courage, and move past the small ego-identity. They move to their own larger life awareness—like a light bulb going on in an epiphany! One moment of self-discovery opens the door to the awareness that self-discovery is our true life's purpose.

Your story becomes a key in the door when it shows how people move towards the deeper value and past the old obstructions. We need to fall in love—daily! Your story can give a recipe for recreating principles that work.

> *If something diminishes you, just move past it.*
> *Try doing nothing in the midst of emotions. Wait to emerge again.*
> *Find your courage to forgive.*
> *Find your courage to deepen love.*

Mamma Mia and Rumi

Have Have your seen **Mamma Mia**, the rollicking, foolish, musical movie of several seasons ago? A few seasons ago, I watched it on a plane flight to Canada. It's a silly movie in many respects, but as soon as you translate the story about love and people's fears and objections to love into 'Universal Metaphor Language,' you will find some great insights. My favorite part was a song in the movie, "Take a chance on me!" This is a line that the great spiritual poet Rumi would have happily used.

In the song, you hear a call for courage. An older spinster confronts an aging, lonely bachelor about the possibility of raising the standards of life much higher, beyond their private and singular loneliness habits. She urges him—and also herself—to strike out past all fear into the territory of real love!

The song will sing in your brain for weeks, and rightfully so, because our inner awareness system really understands this clear metaphor well. We all have old constrictions—small fears or gremlins that have held on for too long. It is time to bust loose from the traps of old self-pity into the territory of true freedom!

Methinks this song cuts far too close to the truth for those of us, (all of us), facing the various value challenges that hit our communities or, for that matter, any other crises of faith. The song calls us to courage.

All of us need to hear the inner challenge to keep raising our eyes to the call of love. How many coaching newsletters from how many coaching schools have fluttered electronically past my eyes in the last years, with the aim of counseling and consoling the fearful?

Meanwhile, the real call, Mother Earth's call, and the World Game's call, is a wake-up call! "Take a chance on me!" Will we give our hearts to what is truly important to us?

- What comfort zones are we willing to move past in the name of real love?

- *What gifts and legacies are we willing to give for our children and their future?*

"Take a chance on me" calls the song! What does Love want from you now, at this point in life? This is the opportunity for creating a World Game!

- *What boldness now, as the planet creaks with seven billion of us?*
- *What vision now, while so many quake in their boots about job challenges and the lowering of the income level? Or about cultural or environmental challenges?*

And so, my friends, I invite you and challenge you to really take on the World Game as an opportunity for true leadership. Take a chance to let your vision free! Take a chance on your own courage to actively move to life affirmation with your own creative enterprise.

What do you want to do with this one wild and wonderful life? Move beyond the fear of dreaming! How do you want a chance to let your heart free! What small sacrifices in comfort could allow you to expand your range of inner freedom and truth?

Move beyond all victim identification and meet the heart's message!

What chance do you want to take to let your voice free! What skills as a coach do you sit on for fear of upsetting people? Move beyond fear of conflict! Offer what you have!

Old Mother Earth offers her best. Life dazzles us with amazing opportunities. What World Game purpose might truly light up your inner vision?

What do you truly want to take a chance on?

Commit yourself! Allow your World Game vision to become a pathway that you follow relentlessly. Let your vision have wings so that you fly fearlessly towards the call of your inner life. In Rumi's words: "Even if you have broken your vow a thousand times. Come, yet again, come, come!" Take a wonderful chance on love's purpose becoming **your** purpose!

What Kinds of Principles Are Transformational?

Assist people to find their own fundamental principles by building simple reframes that express a deep purpose. What kind of principles might you show people discovering?

In the stories within this book, you hear of people recognizing important values and developing linkages to inner principles. For your own stories, find images of learning and development that provoke inner question and further self-exploration. Notice the examples in this book. We are exploring principles:

- of **Balance** (*Karl Wallenda*)
- of **Compassion** (*Mother Teresa*)
- of **Forgiveness** (*Mohandas Gandhi*)
- of **Truth Exploration** (*The Hermit*)
- of **Courage** (The River *Crossing*)
- of **Coach Position** (*The Tonglin Monk*)
- of **Compelling Purpose** (*David Rigmore*)

Build a metaphor that asserts a strong value. Give your listeners a clear image of how they can engage deeply with their life and how things can truly become different.

Mother Teresa's Rules

This famous set of principles—often called **Mother Teresa's Rules** because she loved them—has been quoted in many places. Created by Kent Keith, this rolling set of principles is a great example of a punch line that serves!

Do It *Anyway*

People are often unreasonable, illogical, and self-centered.
Forgive them anyway.

If you are kind, people may accuse you of selfish, ulterior motives.
Be kind anyway.

If you are successful, you will win some false friends and some true enemies.
Succeed anyway.

If you are honest and frank, people may cheat you.
Be honest and frank anyway.

What you spend years building, someone could destroy overnight.
Build anyway.

If you find serenity and happiness, they may be jealous.
Be happy anyway.

The good you do today, people will often forget tomorrow.
Do good anyway.

Give the world the best you have and it may just never be enough.
Give the world the best you have anyway.

You see, in the final analysis, it's all between you and God.
It was never between you and them anyway.

— Kent Keith

Create Presence

You can use your metaphor to build **presence**. Your story becomes powerful when you create presence.

Value descriptions open the awareness of our own deeply associative inner truth. Elicit an outcome—perhaps a principle that honors the experience of self-awareness and truth-awareness. Show the inner experience: how the person in the story realizes that he or she has a choice or is moving in the direction that honors that choice.

If your audience tends to stay stuck in the past, your story will bring them into '**now awareness**.' Through your images, you can move them to a transformational moment of presence (present tense) and to an unfolding future. You create a transformational shift from an old storyline to new engaging experience in every story that you tell.

It is often useful to let the old belief set the original context for the emergent transformation. The story of "Marie and the Shock Treatments" is a good example. Describe the old belief and the feelings and sensations associated with the old belief. Notice the listener's typical body experience as they hear the story—the one that occurs when the listener is experiencing that belief. Notice the self-referenced bundle of difficult thoughts that accompanies this experience. Then, point to how that can open and change in the story. In the story "Milton and George," we saw Milton Erickson do this in his preparations to spend a morning with George, in a back ward of the Worcester State Mental Hospital in Massachusetts. He put himself in George's position and developed his plan based on George's habitual old beliefs.

Use an opening that simply shows the old incident or habit as one snippet of life's journey. For example: *"People sometimes experience their life as if they are stuck."* Then, contrast this with other values, attitudes, and living experiences that open the doorway to life renewal. The aim is to elaborate the context and the shapes, sounds, and core values of transformed awareness within the movement of the story. Shift to describe the expanded presence, inner freedom, and a capacity to engage with inner and outer life in a way that shows much larger awareness.

Elaborate the transformed potential and show it as easily available. Describe the shifted visuals, the enlarged awareness through the body, and the engaged inner values with which the listeners are now connecting. Describe how this transformative vision gives so much more. They now have another way to experience all areas of their life. Make it long-term, something they will want to keep and develop for themselves.

The Story of Tommy the Hermit

There I was, among tall Saguaro cactuses, big boulders, and big craggy mountain peaks, on a trail winding over hill and dale, from grassy open areas to deep canyons. I spent three days in some of the most isolated, yet astounding, wilderness in North America—the Superstition Mountains of rural Arizona—with only a small backpack, a large waterskin, and a well-thumbed map. I had not seen another person for two days. It was time to find a camp for my third night in the open so I turned off on a small meandering trail towards a treed area at the base of a rugged cliff front beside the mountain, about half a mile away.

As I entered the treed area, I was amazed to see large, round, white stones lined up on each side of the path. Suddenly, I moved through a canopy of branches, and walked into a well-organized open camp with several tents and fire pits. I was in someone's home!

A very small man, with big eyes, a warm smile, and a grizzled beard, came towards me. He was dwarf-sized, and looked up at me through shaggy locks of red hair. He extended his hand… "Tommy's the name!"

Somewhat shocked by his presence, let alone by his size and appearance, I introduced myself as if this was an expected occasion. He chose to treat my appearance as a happy surprise: "You're my first visitor in 10 years," he announced. "Would you have dinner with me?"

Picture two, rather surprised human beings sitting by the fire in the deep wilderness, eating beans and drinking coffee, glad to see each other. The meeting was indeed an astonishing event. What happened next? I relaxed and listened to Tommy's stories. He talked about 15 years of hunting for The Lost Dutchman Gold Mine. "See all those holes in the mountain over there?" He was proud of his achievements: "Didn't find the Lost Dutchman Mine yet, but I'm going to. This is the right spot to dig!"

He was talkative: he didn't ask me much about myself, but shared story after story. He showed me the verses of the Bible he had been copying, in large script, for his mother in Louisiana who was nearly blind.

"She depends on me to send her Bible verses that she can read," he said, "and she is funding my expedition. She sends me a check every two months, and I go out for grub and mail her some verses. When I find the gold, she is going to have a happy retirement."

His comments puzzled me but I accepted them. I thought that, for him, his task and his role was totally legitimate, and his solitary life had a real function. I thought to myself, "Well now, I get to meet a really strange one!"

So now I knew the plot. Shortly, he knew mine: touring the wild country for a short 'get to know myself,' 'get to know the land,' and 'get to know real silence' vigil. That puzzled him, but he accepted it. Obviously, to him, I was also a 'strange one.'

Picture the scene: two strange ones, talking together, and pleased for a chance to celebrate simply being human, each one being courteous about the other's strangeness. There they sat, on a star-spangled night in the middle of the wilderness: one campfire and two humans, enjoying the beans, each one listening to the other, from a model of the world that seemed totally different from the other's inner world.

There was not a lot to say, but we found a way to say it. He told me about the birds, the insects, and the lizards. I listened, and asked questions about the tame pigeons that cooed softly as they were roosting in the netting above his head. "My friends," he said.

I expressed enthusiasm for the mountains and he radiated pleasure. I listened as he spoke with pride about his friends, the birds, and his 'home' in the wilderness. I respected his energy and his resourcefulness. **Neighbors can be neighborly anywhere!**

I showed him my worn map and expressed a few travel concerns. He expressed assurance that I would be safe on the return journey. I relaxed, listening to his travel tips and hearing his friendly tone.

We talked about the amazing array of stars visible from the high country. "Yup," he said, "God is sure present out here." I nodded. Together, we noticed the wholeness, and shared the experience of beauty and blessing. **Neighbors can be neighborly anywhere!**

What is a neighbor anyway? I turned in to my sleeping bag, assured of safety and friendship from an odd stranger. He turned into his own quarters, having been visited by a real friend. I no longer thought of him as a strange-looking hermit, but rather as a member of the mighty clan of my friends. I began to envision a worldwide clan of friends—people who assist each other in rebuilding their faith in themselves by offering basic human assistance and warmth when needed, no matter how surprising the encounter. **Neighbors can be neighborly anywhere!**

I headed back the next morning, never to return. Tommy occasionally surfaces in my thoughts to this day. The experience gave me a perspective on the nature of human friendship that I had never considered before. There is no such thing as a hermit, and nobody lives alone. Humanity allows no corner to hide in.

> *We are all in this together. One planet. One humanity. We must love one another or die.*

Unbroken Wholeness: A Meditation

There is an unbroken wholeness that contains us all, like an envelope.

Breathe this wholeness into your awareness, expanding your sight and hearing. Expand this awareness far beyond your normal range—expanding attention way, way, out and far above your body, so you experience your *tingling peripheral awareness*. Allow this awareness to grow tenfold. Float your attention out, like opening an expanding umbrella.

Open your umbrella of awareness to the periphery of the known universe and feel the wholeness. Keep opening even further into the expansive blue sky of deep awareness and into the endlessness of living intelligence.

Relax deeply and float. Notice that you are larger than 100 billion suns, yet you can float and enjoy. *Be* the universe. Feel yourself emerging into wakefulness here, the way you begin to emerge from dreams in the morning. Feel the loving embrace of life holding you in its expansive heart. Float for a while in this texture. Enjoy the experience of awakening into unbroken presence. Become this true awareness.

Chapter 12

Soaring With Synchronicity

Truth is how the creation works.
—William Blake

Beyond Belief: The Power of Synchronicity

We need to celebrate synchronicities. The brain is local. The mind is non-local. Synchronicities remind us of this in many surprising ways. My life journey seems to be designed to show me this again and again.

Synchronicities and promises dwell together. If we hope for something big, do we then dare to promise to make it real? When we promise something big, the world often seems to conspire to assist us with all kinds of material and emotional aid.

Here is an example of a 'simple synchronicity' involving three separate synchronicities inside one round-trip event. All three assisted my capacity to keep a big promise. The first part, which happened in Istanbul, a city of fifteen million people, is wonderful in itself.

Planning to fly to Korea round-trip on a 'less than well-known' airline, I learned that I would be charged 750 euros extra for overweight luggage, for each leg of the trip—a substantial additional cost for one passenger. A woman, who I had met a few hours earlier, just 'happened to know' someone in the airline's ticketing department in Istanbul. She quickly made a telephone call to plead my case as a person worthy of exemption. Through her efforts, an overweight exemption was granted. With strong gratitude, I made the journey!

A week later in Seoul, Korea, a city of eight million, I was just about to leave for the airport for my return trip to Paris when I remembered I would be on the very same airline as before. Once again, I would face the same overweight luggage issue. I was now in a large seminar room, almost alone, having just said goodbye to sixty people. Inwardly, I scolded myself for having forgotten this airline challenge and leaving it to the last moment.

At that point, I inwardly 'wished' to the universe that I had another 'angel,' like the woman in Istanbul, to handle my overweight luggage. Clearly, I sent an inner message from 'Seoul to Soul' because the result was not just one, but two synchronicities. The first happened immedi-

ately. Just at that moment, a woman came through the door, saying she wanted to give me her business card before I left. You guessed it! Of all people in Seoul, Korea, she both spoke English and was, according to the title on her business card, an 'Airlines Consultant.' Amazingly, she knew the Seoul director of the airline for which my ticket was purchased and, within five minutes, the director agreed to arrange an exemption for my overweight luggage. As you can imagine, I threw forth thoughts of great gratitude as I drove to the airport.

The next synchronicity happened at the airport. While explaining my kilo exemption to the ticket agent at the check-in wicket, I accidentally pulled out and handed her the wrong business card, not the one given to me by the Airlines Consultant, but that of another member of my class. The ticket agent looked startled as she read the card in Korean.

The overweight situation was quickly sorted out as someone called the airline director to confirm my exemption. Still, the ticket agent thoughtfully observed the business card I had handed her, and asked me about myself. I briefly explained that I had been teaching Solution-Focused Coaching in Seoul, and that the woman on the business card had been in a student in my course. "I know her well," said the young woman, in faltering English. "I was thinking about her just before you came to me. I honor her so much. She has changed my life. We are in a small health circle together. We were once both very ill. She has regained her health, and now really helps me with my health. And you are teaching her!"

One hour later, face flushed, she was at the plane's entry line with me, and shook my hand just before I was about to board the plane. She had upgraded me to first class, and I found myself in a wonderful, fully furnished sleeping compartment for the long flight. Great gratitude!

Just another synchronicity? I seem have a life full of them! Perhaps you do too, but do not notice them. You might say to me that some people just have lucky lives. Maybe, maybe more—much more!

The brain is local. The mind is non-local. Our lives are wonderfully mysterious! Synchronicities provide a delicious 'shock therapy' that

> reminds us to stay awake to the deep mystery, to stay deeply grateful for the surprises that life sends to us, and to give back the amazing love that life gives to us.

Identity as a Field of Consciousness

Our identity ideas access our common *field of consciousness*—a deep metaphor about what it means to be human. Our identity, as a metaphor, is like a library card to our own personal 'reading room' in our library of consciousness. If our identity remains unexamined, it remains small and barricaded behind walls of old stories and concepts. We can easily remain, for a lifetime, in a *rigid room* with carefully held, non-negotiable boundaries, walls, and conclusions. Necessarily, any person living inside such a personal *small room* keeps his or her life story filled with endless emotional simplifications and often finds feelings of despondency and inner conflict.

We can always expand our metaphors and even get a *library card* for the entire *library of life* if we explore deeply, or if someone simply shows us how to find and open the door. We then become truly interested in expanded awareness because we become cognizant of the inner qualities, the rich openings into grace and self-renewal.

On a deep level, we all know what inner transformation is. We can notice how our strongest metaphors offer a library card to transformational awareness. Asking open-ended questions and listening with care, we find ways to use this card effectively.

Learning how to connect with a field of value can be a major theme in a story with strong transformational potency. As coaches, we can demonstrate the principles of opening an inner door to real life renewal.

Your story can offer this if you:
- Choose a transformational field relevant to your listeners.
- Call upon your inner power to express that deep relevance.
- Begin your story by connecting yourself to the core values that the story exemplifies.

- Demonstrate the power of inner connection, both to vision and value, to self and listeners.
- Include sensory description, tonal shift, and body language of reconnection and realignment.
- Ask inwardly to express that deep relevance. Your inner request is like a prayer that can open into passionate expression as you speak.

From your own perspective, you will find the ability to express the emergent principles of self-trust and trust in others to be like wings for your story. You take flight into expressive power.

A personal identity can easily become very narrow if it is only an emotional identity built from comparing the *self* to others. It might even be described as a *thought virus* and like any virus, it keeps us in *invasion fighting* mode.

We want to move the listener beyond the *old* internal dialogue of *self-divisions*. We want to move the listener beyond personal identity as self-aggrandizement, and especially beyond self-entitlement and the *right* to be offended. We are expanding from narrow self-protection into our wider awareness.

The Cave

Have you experienced a great miracle? Perhaps you recall a moment when life's gifts appear in great array and you are awed and amazed by what you have received. One such moment happened many years ago, on a two-day hike I took with my 12-year-old daughter, 8-year-old son, his best friend, and the family dog. I carried our one backpack, which contained a very small, light tent and enough food for the four of us for two days. Our aim was to create a pleasant overnight camp along a rather difficult trail on the West Coast of British Columbia, Canada, and to return the next day. It was a first-time experience for the boys.

It was mid-August and we had experienced hot weather for two weeks straight. We started out early in the morning and had a fun-filled day. We were, at best, several hours from our planned campsite when the weather changed dramatically. A sudden storm, accompanied by the rumble of thunder, flowed in from the ocean; and a strong wind began to blow, bringing big drops of rain. A wind arose, and the sky darkened ominously.

We were on a narrow, deeply shaded trail, filled with huge trees and undergrowth. There was nowhere to camp. Realizing that we might be in trouble, I followed the first tiny animal trail I could find which led down towards the ocean. I was looking for a bit of flat ground to pitch our tiny tent, but all that surrounded me was dense brush, trees, and steep slopes.

The thunder continued, the growl getting closer. After ten minutes of carefully trekking downhill, we found a small bay but were disappointed to discover that it was piled high with logs that had been washed ashore, and that there was no flat ground except at the water's edge. Meanwhile, the storm was beginning to look serious, with huge flashes of lightning and menacing sheets of rain moving quickly toward us.

The children joked on the beach. Meanwhile, I was running back and forth, hunting for kindling and a decent spot to pitch our tent. I was a bit desperate and inwardly requested help. There were maybe only five dry minutes left.

A large jumble of logs was pushed directly against the rock wall at the back of the small beach and tiny bay. I started climbing the heap, trying to find a sheltered spot between the logs and the unrelenting rock face of the shoreline, but I had no luck. Reaching the top of one of the log jams, I came right up to the granite face against which the logs were pitched. Moving carefully along the logs near the rock facade, I suddenly saw a 'tent door' sized niche in an area near the base of the rock, yet high above the bay. It was concealed behind some of the logs. A waist-high opening was available, but almost invisible from below. In desperation, I peered in, and to my surprise found that the space immediately widened into a rather large, room-sized, dry cave with a flat floor.

Calling the kids to gather all of the wood we could find, before everything was completely wet, we pulled stacks of logs, branches, and wood chips under the small overhang at the cave mouth. We all moved inside just as the full force of the storm hit with sheets of lightning, pouring water, and big winds. I have rarely seen such a raging storm.

Dry and out of the wind, we removed our wet outer garments and lit a small fire near the cave's mouth. As we warmed up, we appreciated the amazing place we were in: a room-like cave about nine meters wide and five meters deep. It was completely dry and flat, with an incredible back wall covered in native hieroglyphs—arrows, circles, dots, and figures. The drawings looked very old. The cave felt friendly and actually homey. We cooked our food, read, and sang songs, in the full spirit of the camping adventure. We laid out our sleeping bags and slept, dry and warm.

In the morning, we discovered the storm was still strong, with rain pelting down relentlessly over the bay. Half a meter away from us, the world was drenched. We sat by our fire, read aloud, played games, and enjoyed the morning. Around noon, the storm suddenly stopped, the sun emerged, and the four of us, safe and dry, started our walk back to the end of the trail where the family car awaited us.

You can imagine my thoughts walking back. **Wonderful unexpected moments to share together are truly miracles, are they not?** The children saw the event not as a miracle, but as a natural part of their day and life. They accepted it simply, in a way that amazed me. They helped me realize that most of life seemed like magic to them. Their version was: "Oh, now this is the part of the trip where we wait in a cave and have fun, out of the rain."

I, however, knew it was a spectacular gift. In a coastline without caves, a cave had appeared. In a situation without solution, a solution had appeared. The storm could have presented major problems for us. What joy the miracle of the cave had produced! You look, you ask, you pray for help, and you find! Something, never encountered in any of my previous experiences, shows itself in a moment of absolute need. Surprising synchronicity! How wonderful are the miraculous gifts that life offers us.

> **Little miracles are still miracles, are they not?**
> Life's generosity is such a miracle.
> **Wonderful unexpected moments to share together are truly miracles, are they not?**
> Life's generosity is truly a miracle.
>
> Scientists have estimated that 99% of life's experiences are positive for people no matter what they say or think. Turn your attention to life's miracles.

Use Open-Ended Questions as Punch Lines

Questions make wonderful punch lines. Every story can hold a punch line question! A great story shows the process of discovering one's deeper questions and further development of those questions. Just pick a theme and explore the limitless possibilities.

All people want to learn how to say *yes* to their experiences. We first show their difficulty as a question and then we show their question in action, as a larger human question. This allows the listener to find his or her own unique response.

With a *punch line question*, we are aiming for inspiration. We ask ourselves: "*What might we say to a person that would inspire them for the rest of their lives?*" The story "The Eagle" ends with variations on such a question.

There is a great question for 'setting your space' as you begin to express your metaphor to others: "*What is the largest identity I can think through as I tell this story?*"

Our larger self has multiple aspects. Find a wide viewpoint that is coherent and inclusive, and take your listeners into that experience.

What is the larger self? Step into your *life of value*. Our expansion system connected to value is much larger than our narrow personal identity theories. We can tap into a much wider logic system and perceptual mode that widens our awareness far beyond our normal self-references. This is like building a rocket launch system designed to lift us beyond the atmospheric drag of the small, very personal mind.

The Eagle

We all have indelible moments: memorable occasions that live, like video clips in our inner vision, for a lifetime and become imprinted into our Being. **Life gives us gifts**, does it not? These memories are enormously important to the warmth and camaraderie that we show each other along the journey.

I invite you to imagine a misty sunrise on the rocky coast of the Pacific Ocean. See a small, sandy beach bounded by huge conifers. I am on the third wonderful day of a hike, solo, along the Pacific Coast, and I have several more days of hiking to complete my journey on this rugged trail. See me, Marilyn Atkinson walking, stretching, and folding my sleeping bag to start the day.

Down the bay from where I had camped that night, I noticed that an elderly Native American fisherman had pulled up a small, white fishing boat and had a fire going on the beach. The smell of coffee wafted in my direction and when he saw my approach on the beach, he held up a cup and beckoned me over. Without a word, he handed me the cup of coffee.

Grateful for the hot drink on a wet morning, I sat and sipped quietly while he knelt beside the fire and smoked. Finally, he stood up, pointed to the native village across the bay, and said, "I am going there. Do you want a ride?"

Realizing that this would put me half a day closer to a delightful part of my journey, I agreed and we got into the boat. Moving out slowly, several miles into the bay, he pointed to the mountains, now clearly in view. He drew my attention to the tops of each of seven high hills around the bay. There were seven bald eagles, each perched on a bare branch of the highest tree of each hill. They were barely visible, yet clearly present.

I was amazed at seeing them all there, the seven guardians of the seven mountains. "They are all watching us," he said. **Life gives us gifts**, and I was experiencing one of them.

Noticing my strong interest, he cautions to me, "Sit and don't move! Watch this." He stuck his hand into a large box of freshly caught fish. He chose a big red snapper and weighed it in his hands. Then he stood up, held the fish high, and faced the nearest eagle, which was over one mile away.

Then he rotated his arm clockwise three times and tossed the fish high in the air. It landed with a smacking sound in the water near the boat. As soon as the fish hit the water, the eagle launched off its tree branch. With smooth, strong wing strokes, the eagle flew towards us, as fast as an arrow.

I was amazed at the speed of the giant bird. I was in awe of its one and one-half-meter wingspan, and the speed of its flight straight towards our boat. As I watched, it dove towards us. I saw its bright beady eyes.

Hovering, it extended its claws like landing gear, and spread its talons wide. In one smooth, silent swoop, it reached through and picked up the large red fish that floated just below the water's surface. Its wings beat furiously, as the eagle dragged the fish out of the water and stared fiercely at me, two meters away the entire time. Slowly, the eagle lifted off with its prize, soared high into the air, and sped back to its mountain top perch.

I was speechless. The sight still lives in my memory: the white head, the proud eyes, the shining wings, the ballet of motion—a vision never to be forgotten.

The old man laughed at my amazement. "Something to see, eh?" he said, while starting the boat's engine. Five minutes later, quietly, as if to himself, he repeated it lovingly again, under his breath: "Yes. Really something to see!"

Nothing more needed to be said as we crossed the bay.

Oh, friends everywhere, notice how **life gives us gifts, wonderful gifts**. We get them when we least expect them, do we not? We learn so much from generous strangers, do we not? What shining moments do we create for others in return? What generosity do we generate in ourselves in return? What aims do we foster to celebrate the wonderful gifts of life?

To move free, we need to build strong visual awareness and also strong inner trust—opening self-awareness until we can float in overview in an expansive, observational orbit. This ties to questioning '*beyond the beyond*' until we build a nervous system that matches. We can then enjoy the vast stability of self-realization. The following meditation gives an example.

A Meditation—Catching the Breath of the Universe: Big and Small

You will find this meditation a useful practice of visual movement toward enlightenment.

It requires that you visualize your entire life, past, present, and future as if it were a line representing all the sequenced events of your past personal existence as well as your future possibilities. Give the line some of your own unique personal qualities to signify your unique ownership.

Some people see their line as a shining thread, some as a pathway, and others see it as a stream or flow of color or brightness. Float far up above your timeline and relax into a *coach* or *observer* perspective. See all of it below you. Notice that if you go far enough above, you can experience this viewpoint as large and the timeline as small. It does not make any difference whether you experience short, eye-blink visuals of different images or stable pictures in a beautiful line. Just relax, and observe what you see spread out below.

From the albums of *life videos* on your timeline, take note of yourself in various typical situations, and in various cultural and personal frameworks common to yourself. Notice any typical habits where you enact various mundane or habitual fixations, actions, or even points of narrowed awareness. Just observe a variety of small scenarios. Be totally appreciative of that person who has been you, so busy in his or her life that he or she didn't notice some areas becoming closed, and hence became habituated to various postures, beliefs, or physical and/ or emotional habits.

Become relaxed, compassionate, and accepting as you observe a few habits typical of this *personal memory system* you are observing. Watch the ideas of *yourself* that you are accustomed to, and take time to see some of the habitual responses in various typical situations. If you tend to be unforgiving of your behavior in some contexts, forgive yourself for those behaviors. Remember the vast varieties of wonderful responses, activities, postures, openness, compassion, and fun qualities that this person—you—is also capable of showing and experiencing.

Next—imagine that your timeline shrinks to a very tiny image. So, as an *expanded universal being*, you can reach down and pick up this tiny timeline, like an energy item, and place it softly in the viewing space before you, so you can observe it. See the line, itself, as bright light.

Observe quite impartially this timeline that represents your entire life. Once again, notice the timeline as an *energy item*. Notice that you can see the energy of the whole item named '*your life's memories.*'

Now—maintaining this relaxed coach or observer position, now switch focus. Become aware of the huge, energetic spaciousness around this timeline expanding out, forever and ever into the cosmos. Feel this enormous expanding energy of luminous space, both in front and behind your timeline. Experience the qualities that represent this spacious energy.

Note your visualization of the enormity of the universe—thoughtfully watching from an observation point that sees it all. How do you see it? Perhaps you see the universe as blackness, perhaps as a blue softness, or as emptiness or lightness. Wonder at its hugeness, its energy, and its openness. Is there a sound that accompanies what is universal?

In your own way, become aware of the sacredness and purity of this endless space, and relax as you observe and experience into it further and further. Take time to expand your view out—ten times as far again—seeing the universe as a vast periphery of aliveness and richness of possibility, becoming aware of the quality of its infinite wholeness and energy.

You may see this awesome endless openness any way you like: as round or flat, as bright or dark, as luminous or velvety, shimmering, or still. Perhaps see it as a huge awareness. Perhaps start to notice how this robust expanding space surrounding all is like a vast mother, providing an endless universal energy to your own small timeline. Allow yourself to become playful with the vision in any way you want. Sense the energy.

Once again, go back to your own small timeline: this tiny item suspended in this universal energy. Again, begin seeing your small line like a tiny energy item in this enormity of energy around it. Notice and sense the vastness, like a huge vessel or container.

As if you were that huge mother, be tenderly *okay* with all that you have noticed about your own small *life memory* item.

Observe the two together—big and small. The objective is to go back and forth between big and small, noticing first one, then the other. Gradually notice that you can see the energy of the two together: the vast, open energy of space and the particular, unique energy of your tiny personal timeline.

Begin to notice the two together as two parts of a whole. Notice how, in some way, they show a resonance and an inner awareness of each other. Notice their sameness. In your own way, see each as whole and also a vessel. Ask yourself to *understand* the inner qualities that could be the same between them. Then ask, "*What essence do they share?*"

Become aware of the growing awareness between your own tiny timeline and the vast, open energy of space surrounding it, and begin to see connection and interpenetration between them. Perhaps you can begin to notice a slight movement in your small timeline, like a *breathing* or *vibration*, and notice the huge universal energy as responding in harmony.

Imagine metaphors for the resonance and interaction between them:

- the tiny timeline, like a small capsule vibrating in an oceanic space of rapture
- movement between them like a dance, both sharing the same inner rhythms
- together as endless swirls of light—your timeline a bright spark in the larger cosmos
- two harmonious sounds in a sweet, endlessly echoing chord
- two processes—tenderly touching or tingling together

Notice the energy of the small timeline gradually begin to resonate completely with the universal energy. Notice the totally natural quality of this resonance as a form of perfection or a form of sacredness. Choose your own unique visual metaphor for sacred interaction.

Observe them together for a while, in the free space of your own personal visual imagery, gently appreciating their inner connection to each other and their total resonance together.

Now, once again, move in closer to the timeline where you can observe the details of this—your life. Notice that when you look into the line, and *open up* any particular moment in the line, you can notice the natural rhythm and resonance of universal sacred energy pervading all aspects of any particular moment you observe. Observe moments which you previously had only seen as mundane, and notice the sacred quality of the inner connection pervading all aspects like a deep luminosity of inner connectedness.

Take some relaxed time to simply view some various moments past, present, or future, and observe the light and learning in all you see. Allow yourself to notice and enjoy the sacred resonance in each moment into which you look. Notice how genuine sacred qualities pervade all aspects and how deep learning, discovery, and inner connection can now be seen as the primary field for all action *in life*.

When you are ready, visualize yourself moving *back down* inside the timeline and into this moment of *your own day and life now*.

Take a moment to feel the resonance, the sacred space of awareness—*only now from the inside*. Sense the sacredness in your own body. Sense the sacredness in the moment. Take a relaxed breath and experience gratitude for the vast resonance, the space of awareness of which you are a part.

Look at objects around you and, through your own capacity, notice the deep awareness that pervades the space you are in right at this moment. And, with this, sense your body, your blood flow, and your inner experience as a powerful doorway to the heart of this universal vibration of which you partake.

Chapter 13

Awareness, Presence, and Wisdom

A hundred times every day I remind myself that my inner and outer life are based on the labors of other men, living and dead, and that I must exert myself in order to give in the same measure as I have received and am still receiving...

—Albert Einstein

The Solution-Focused Power of Gratitude

Every year—usually as we draw towards the end—many of us take time to express appreciation to our colleagues, our friends, and our families. This annual ritual has led me to think about the nature of true appreciation. Strong thinkers have spoken well on this subject.

Melody Beattie:

Gratitude unlocks the fullness of life. It turns what we have into enough and plenty. It turns denial into acceptance, chaos to order, and confusion to clarity. Appreciation is most powerful when it is prompt, heartfelt, specific to an event, and designed to highlight a shining moment for someone. In other words, appreciation, at its best, is designed to light up a person's day! It can turn a meal into a feast, a house into a home, a stranger into a friend. Gratitude makes sense of our past, brings peace for today, and creates a vision for tomorrow.

A great example of appreciation I once received came from a woman who artfully painted designs on my ink-stained business jacket to make it look like designer fashion. As I took the cap off a black felt pen in front of a class, ink had sprayed my light beige suit with black marks. I discarded the jacket, assuming it would go into the trash. The next morning, the woman handed my jacket back to me—elegantly painted. Her words were simply: "*Thank you so much for this seminar.*" It became a favorite garment that I was able to wear for years.

Another wonderful example occurred when someone wrote a song and dance routine designed to highlight the end of a fun-filled program. It was amazing and inspired. We boogied to the music, and my heart began to sing. Her humorous efforts at gratitude lit up my whole week.

The benefits of appreciation, of course, are not limited to the recipient. Often the act of appreciation is of even greater benefit to the person extending the offer. Health statistics show that silent appreciative prayer or thought or invocation for something you appreciate is good for the heart. Studies show that '*saying grace*' or expressing gratitude for a meal allows for the food to be more savored and even aids in digestion. Saying grace is not about religion. It is about acknowledging our deep connection to those with whom we partake and acknowledgement of the labor that we *receive* as a result of what has been prepared for us. Our gratitude towards life in general opens our capacity for presence and wisdom.

When the power of gratitude is fully understood, it opens the door for understanding. For example, when we acknowledge the full extent of the loving labor each parent performed for us— their child—it allows us to declare gratitude for all their past efforts and thus, we achieve peace and unity with our parents.

Appreciation builds a virtuous circle. It is like an ocean liner creating an outgoing wave leading to even more value, and acknowledgement for everyone in its wake.

The tone of blessing is a big part of solution-focused coaching as well. Effective coaching is appreciative. As coaches, we appreciate our clients fully, in the same way we listen to them fully. Through our efforts, they experience added self-esteem and self-awareness. Their gratitude is our reward.

The Village of Shining Moments

I recently heard a story from the middle ages, about a weary traveler approaching a village on foot after crossing the mountains. He had stopped near the village graveyard to eat his lunch. While chewing his food, he noticed some of the dates on the gravestones and realized that all the stones he saw indicated lifetimes of only two, three, or four years. "Strange," he thought. Before he continued his journey, he walked through the graveyard looking more closely at the dates. To his amazement, he discovered that no tombstone marked an age greater than five years.

Determined to discover what this meant, he walked to the village, where he saw clearly there were people of all ages. Asked about the graveyard, people laughed and, without comment, sent him to the village elder. Ever more curious, he followed their directions. He waited patiently to see this elder, willing and ready for this mystery to be revealed. An old man with a kindly chuckle finally emerged with tea in hand, and they sat together and talked.

> *"We in our village have a secret agreement," he said. "We only want to register as our 'lifetime moments' those particular moments that have been the most alive, vital, and real for us—those moments that we have filled with value! We all love life here! We appreciate life's value and take it very seriously. For this reason, we have agreed to play a game called 'living life at its best.' We agree to carefully note our inner truth about the quality of real life. For this purpose, carefully note down our best life moments every day and carefully accrue them.*
>
> *"We seek these moments with each other to make sure we truly live them: shining moments of discovery, value, and inner truth, or significant shared experiences that we deeply recognize. These are our real lives, and these we honor as our true lifetime. It is a wonderful task to create these moments. We encourage them in each other. We gather them like a harvest and share them in 'winter moments' to extend them.*
>
> *"Our gravestones tell our story: We are the village of shining moments! Each one of us can find moments of truth and beauty and give our presence to them. Each one of us can live in moments of truth and beauty—even this very moment—if we want to. This moment is different from any before it. This moment is different… it's **now**."*
>
> *What is this shining moment for you? Breathe deep and experience your presence now. What is this shining moment for you? What makes it extraordinary? Feel the tingling awareness in your hands. What is this shining moment for you? Hear all the sounds around you, merging into the far distant reaches. This moment is different from any before it. This moment is different. It is **now**.*

The Meaning of 'Field Awareness'

What does *field awareness* actually refer to in the context of *metaphor creation*? We are describing fields of knowledge that we access when the moment is ripe. These are deep connective bands of awareness that we share together. Think back to the times you have been surprised at the depth of your answers to a really good question.

Someone asks you a strong open-ended question, which leads you to do a trans-derivational search through all time and all locations and come up with the response that is needed. We can open our attention to the subtle knowledge requested and we discover it and speak it eloquently from knowledge that we did not even realize that we possessed.

Physicists use the term *field* to describe frequencies that are beyond physical detection. A transformational field—a quantum matrix is a subtle frequency of awareness. Here we refer to the Latin word *subtle* which means "a finely woven connection."

Essentially, your own *larger awareness* is what is answering such questions. You coherently *come up* with cogent and powerful answers that amaze both you and those around you. In exactly the same way—as you speak—you can use your metaphor to answer key questions and even discover more subtle inner questions emanating from your listeners. If you ask for wider knowledge, the wider and the wiser arrives—just in time.

The Flute Player

Picture a beautiful August day on a mountain near Vancouver. I am hiking on an amazing trail that I've never seen before. It meanders through forests and meadows across the back of a mountain, and I am walking alone, enjoying the wildflowers, the jay birds, and the opportunity to stretch my legs.

I have always been curious about this trail, yet never taken it, which extends from the top of a mountain across toward its back. This day, I am surprised to see that it's quite a small trail. After following it for the first three kilometers, I find that it has been only partially maintained. Now, at this point, I am curiously following the trail down, down, down, twisting and turning, through a forest of large cedar and pine trees. I suspect the low point will be a creek, but I am surprised to discover it is not. The last twenty feet of the trail suddenly steepens and becomes almost vertical, and I slip and slide down, holding onto roots and, suddenly losing my footing, I land on my buttocks in a large clump of grass.

Amazingly, within seconds after I land, another person also falls onto the clump of grass, from the other side of the trail about five feet up and in front of me. The person who slides down the other side is a very handsome young man, dressed in jeans, with a pack on his back. His trail, which I was facing, was just as steep as mine and he also lost his footing and landed in the lush grass at the base. Visualize the two of us, very surprised, sitting face-to-face with each other, almost nose-to-nose.

We both sat there laughing, for a moment. Life has its moments, and this was one of them. Two astonished people!

Now, I am a woman in my sixties and he is a young man, perhaps in his thirties; here we are, each enjoying the joke of landing in the grass. I am about to scramble to my feet, but the young man motions for me to sit for a moment.

Reaching over his shoulder, into his pack, he pulls out a small flute and immediately starts to play. He plays a dancing, silly tune that in some way matches the silliness of the moment. I laugh, relax, and enjoy.

He continues to play, a pretty melody that matches the pretty spot we are in: grass, ferns, and many shades of green. Birds start singing, hearing his flute, and now he matches the bird song also; I relax and listen. Now his music begins to shift and change, widening out as he raises his eyes and looks at the forest. I noticed the sounds now match the Majesty of the big trees around us, strong, tall, deep, gentle, and profound. I sit and listen, really appreciating how well he is touching the quality of the moment. A small celebration starts inside my heart. Oh, pilgrims on the trails of life, **let us listen to each other's music!**

Again the music changes and more sound of celebration begins to emerge. The music widens out, as if it has moved past all the trees and even the forest. Now the flute player is now playing the sky, the clouds, even the reach of space itself.

The music softens, expands, and it is as if the young man, deep in the process, is now beginning to play an appreciation of the whole of life. An exquisite melody emerges, as if the flute is singing in universal gratitude, like a prayer. The sound is wide, deep—a full range of reverent, joyful music.

An arpeggio opens, and the music scales a height of joyful notes, reaching a resounding, celebratory, exquisite hello to all of creation! And then, in one final note of vast, open completion, it dies away. The forest is quiet again.

I sit in awe. Nothing can be said. Nothing needs to be said; the flute has said it all. **Oh, pilgrims, let us listen to each other's music!**

Without a word, the man puts his flute back into its pack. Without a word, I gather myself and rise as he does. Now, like two ancient ones, like samurai, or ancient sages greeting the power of the moment, we both bow and nod to each other.

Then, with nary a word said, he climbs up my side of the trail, and I climb up his.

Oh, brothers and sisters of the moment; oh, coaches of the exquisite power of speaking and listening: enjoy your moments of celebration, and of reaching out to those around you!

Give your gifts in the spirit of awe and joy because we get to share this time with each other. As we receive each other's gifts, the grace of the moment carries us in her arms. Oh, pilgrims, **let us listen to each other's music***. This moment is different from any before it! Share your love!*

Value Awareness

Strive to build metaphors that truly show a person at work, exploring his or her life. The object is to demonstrate a person asking deep open-ended questions, enabling the full use of the mind and fundamental essence of understanding. You want your story to show the process of accessing the expansive field of inner knowledge—the field of value awareness. Let your story reveal what an open-ended question can disclose.

We can describe how the hero of our story gets to the place where he or she knows something to be absolutely valid. In presenting the story, we are asking our listeners to determine what is deeply meaningful for the person in the story, and how does he or she describe and show that inner opening.

In the process of telling our story, we show how people easily access the field of inner value when they ask themselves, "*What is deeply true for me right now?*" We invoke the emergence of wisdom from learning. We are asking the question, "*How does a person turn mundane into sacred?*" These are the ingredients that build a compelling story!

Create Your Own Travel Jar

You may have noticed something special about *transit times*. These are the times you have spent travelling around the world by train, bus, or plane. These times are great opportunities for finding the '*giant stones in the bottle of life*'—the key value areas that we need to keep in focus.

You probably have heard the adage about the multiple bits of gravel in the *Bottle of Life* that use up our time. This old proverb is told again and again in seminars throughout the world. Teachers demonstrate the nature of prioritizing by using a metaphor which describes putting various sizes of stones into a bottle. They show what happens if you don't put the big *core values* stones in first. The moral of this story is that the big core value stones have to go in first because if you fill up the bottle with smaller more insignificant stones, there is no room left in your *bottle of values* at other times in your life. There is so much 'small stuff,' there is no room for what is important.

Travel time provides *downtime* moments to reflect and contemplate:
- What is of prime importance to you?
- What are your big stones?
- What are your core values?
- What is needed to keep your values a primary focus?

Travelling—the actual act of being in transit—has always been a very special one-on-one time for me, myself, and I to bond. When I am in transit, I feel free to explore my own psyche. It's as if the universe opens up its arms and says: "*Okay, you are in my embrace now—free from commitments for the next seven hours of this flight—lots of time to* *focus on what is really important for you to **be** at this point in your life."* Personally, while in transit, I feel free to indulge in the opportunity to stop my work. I move from prose to song, from details to overview, from *doing* to simply *being*. I relax and contemplate, and allow my gratitude to open. I think of my life's events and unique moments, and experience the power and growth of inner value—and it warms my soul. Expanding out to the full reach of life's purpose, we can truly explore our own.

For me, being in transit is a great time to ask the important questions:

- *Is everything all right within my own heart?*
- *How is everything going with my closest people?*
- *How are things going with all my companions?*

Find your own 'quality time' in your life for inner transit—to ask:

- *Who, today, needs gratitude?*
- *Whose courage needs to be recognized?*
- *Whose efforts need to be supported?*
- *Whose loving efforts kindle yours?*
- *What incompletions of major importance exist?*
- *Is anyone dying?*
- *Is anyone truly not available?*
- *How could you knock on their door?*
- *What more can you do to bring gratitude and blessing in the lives of others?*

When in transit or en route, or during your quality time with yourself, don't forget to check your *Travel Jar*—your own *Bottle of Life*. Move from doing to being, and allow your inner jar to be replenished. Promise to refill your jar. Promise to focus on the big stones.

Ask:

- What is deeply important to me?
- What truly important values do I cherish in my life?
- What is my calling?

Develop Field Awareness As You Tell Your Tale

There are multiple key areas for describing and showing *field awareness* throughout a story.

- Feel '*the field*' in your heart and hands so that your listeners deeply recognize your gesture as one that links you to the transformational field you are expressing.
- Link the inner feeling to a *value* word. Say it powerfully, and hear how you say that word, with all attention on its inner meaning.
- Connect to one specific life principle, and speak it clearly at least three times as you tell your story.
- Build the presence of field awareness through your expanded tone of voice and your gestures. "*Let the tone of the wise elder ring forth.*"
- Connect with your aim. If possible, find an open question and deeply ponder it, even as you tell your story.
- Let the story tell itself *through* you.
- Use a slow, open-handed gesture upwards, known as the '*value holding form.*'
- Move your eyes to the mid-distance position between you and the horizon, and hold your eyes in that place where *vision in mind* develops.
- Open your hands and feel the energy in your tingling fingers.

As well, drawing assists others to connect with their own deeper meaning.

- Build drawings that link to your story.
- Use geometric pictures, and link to a vision. Then, speak through that vision.
- Match with rich tonal shifts.

All *field thinking*—by its very nature—links us to **relationship thinking**. Commitment to others is the doorway into a wider *field awareness* that links us all together. It connects us in many different ways. With tone and gesture, we connect to others even as we share our stories. We move from local to non-local mind and enter the tingling present moment with presence.

The Larry Walter's Story

 Many have told the great story of Larry Walters, the wannabe 'airline pilot.' The story is one of courage and breakthrough but is also humorous and wildly creative.

The Larry Walter's story is a tale of reckless self-invention, reminding people that they can jump in and change at any point in their lives. His adventure flying in his lawn chair with 45 helium weather balloons provides great visual images and evocative experience. It has since become the major themes of several movies. People enjoy the idea of Larry sitting in his lawn chair, eating his lunch, peanut butter sandwiches and beer, at 15,000 feet while a Boeing 747 cruises by. We imagine people looking out and watching him as he waves back at them.

I have told this story often, integrating advanced metaphor principles into every part. For example, I always provide a hook for the conscious mind at the beginning—a small bit of dramatic hold!

"You all know Larry. His picture, sitting in his lawn chair, was on the front page of all the world's newspapers back in 1982." Now people listen, and stay glued to the details, curious about whom Larry really was. Why would all the world's newspapers show his picture? They wonder and puzzle... Can I remember that headline?

Telling this story has become a great pleasure for me, because I use it to create easy integration of the story's punch lines into specific principles discussed in a day training program. I link it directly to what I am delivering to the group. This opens the door for group participation and enjoyment.

My favorite is Larry's line, **"Oh Yes!"** when asked if he loved his 24-hour adventure in the flight corridors above the international airport. I have used this simple punch line for many years, to create fun and transformation in a large group. At the end of the Larry story, I will launch with a principle from our day of course work together—whatever the program or group.

> This always inspires a burst of new creative synthesis. I get the group to intone the '**Oh Yes**' punch line with me. I playfully call out "One, two, three," and gesture for them to join in, saying **"Oh Yes"** strongly. We all then do this with evocative, full-bodied gestures and a strong tone.
>
> I find a way for all participants to join in at least three times. Each time, I expand the power of the playful declaration, creating a more and more transformational declaration. Each interaction leads them further, coaxing them to explore their own deep purpose to wake up and find courage and expanded vision. We begin with personal breakthrough, but often end with humanity's breakthrough—feeling it in our bones.

What is a metaphor?

Oh, brothers and sisters of the spirit, we are the creators of transformation in the sacred moments we share together. Oh, let us tell our stories to lead ourselves forward. Let us feel our hearts opening to one another. Let us meet together and create delight in our lives with our stories! Let us say to each other, from the bottom of our toes to the top of our values, **"Oh, Yes!"**

Ohhhh, yes!

Erickson Coaching International

Head Office:

2021 Columbia Street
Vancouver
British Columbia
Canada
V5Y 3V6

1 800 665 6949 (North America)
1 604 879 5600 (Vancouver, BC, Canada)
Fax: 1 604 879 7234
info@erickson.edu
www.erickson.edu

Erickson Coaching International has been expanding programs and courses into about five countries and language groups per year since 2007. In 2013, Erickson Training programs certified by the International Coach Federation were held in 44 countries.

Courses are available on-site and online. Check for the country of your choice. You can also find us on Facebook and LinkedIn.

Armenia	India	Serbia
Australia	Indonesia	Singapore
Barbados	Italy	Slovakia
Brazil	Jamaica	South Korea
Bulgaria	Kazakhstan	Thailand
Canada	Latvia	Tobago
Chile	Lebanon	Trinidad
China	Lithuania	Tunisia
Croatia	Malaysia	Turkey
Cyprus	Norway	Ukraine
Czech Republic	Oman	United Kingdom
Estonia	Poland	United States of America
France	Portugal	Viet Nam
Germany	Romania	
Greece	Russia	

Contact www.erickson.edu to find out more.

Erickson offers the following program about five times a year in locations around the world. To find out more, contact **info@erickson.edu**, or go to **www.erickson.edu** and check under "Where in the world is Marilyn?"

ERICKSON
INTERNATIONAL
Leading since 1980

Dreamwork & Advanced Metaphors

We live metaphoric lives!

Obtain a profound addition to any coach's toolkit for assisting people to explore and expand their abilities. Develop an ear to the stories, internal messages, and belief structures that people use to limit their lives.

What will you learn in this three-day program?

You will learn new methods to listen to your clients' stories and assumptions, and to utilize responsive methodologies that integrate their visions and inner movies with needed choices and changes.

Using vibrant metaphoric processes and exciting Ericksonian techniques, you will learn to build your own powerful metaphors to create compelling visions that inspire people.

The program includes:

- Specific procedures for quickly understanding the unconscious message system and meaning of any dream you may want to explore. You learn to expand your skills as a metaphor creator.

- How-tos for changing inner vision and emotional thought as 'forms of consciousness,' and linking this to enhanced creativity in daily life.

2021 Columbia Street, Vancouver, BC, Canada V5Y 3V6
Telephone: 604-879-5600   Toll-free: 1-800-665-6949
info@erickson.edu   www.erickson.edu

ISBN: 978-0-9783704-3-5

Made in the USA
Monee, IL
18 October 2022